MEDIEVAL POLITICS AND LIFE

Published in 1996 by
Marshall Cavendish Corporation
99 White Plains Road
Tarrytown, NY 10591-9001
U.S.A.

Editor: Henk Dijkstra
Executive Editor: Paulien Retèl
Revision Editor: Henk Singor
Art Director: Henk Oostenrijk, Studio 87, Utrecht, The Netherlands
Index Editors: Schuurmans & Jonkers, Leiden, The Netherlands
Preface: Ellen M. Shortell, Assistant Professor of Art History, Department of Critical Studies, Massachusetts College of Art, Boston

The History of the Ancient and Medieval World is a completely revised and updated edition of
The Adventure of Mankind.
© 1996 HD Communication Consultants BV, Hilversum, The Netherlands
This edition © 1996 by Marshall Cavendish Corporation, Tarrytown, New York and
HD Communication Consultants BV, Hilversum, The Netherlands.

Library of Congress Cataloging-in-Publication Data

History of the ancient and medieval world / edited by Henk Dijkstra.
p. cm.
Completely rev. and updated ed. of: The Adventure of mankind (second edition 1996).
Contents:—v.10. Medieval Politics and Life.
ISBN 0-7614-0361-2 (v.10).—ISBN 0-7614-0351-5 (lib.bdg.:set)
1. History, Ancient—Juvenile literature. 2. Middle Ages—History—Juvenile literature. I. Dijkstra, Henk. II. Title: Adventure of mankind
D117.H57 1996
930—dc20/95-35715

History of the
Ancient & Medieval World

Volume 10

Medieval Politics and Life

Marshall Cavendish
New York   Toronto   Sydney

Medieval Politics and Life

Medieval Garden

CONTENTS

Preface

During the late Middle Ages in Europe the feudal system began to give way to large governments under stronger monarchs. Technology improved agriculture, cloth manufacture, and international trade. The economy was based on money rather than land, and the mercantile class thrived. Peasants bought independence from less wealthy lords. Growing cities throughout Europe were granted a measure of self-government and independence from feudal lords.

Kings increased control by taking the cities under their protection, as in France during the twelfth and thirteenth centuries. In Italy, on the other hand, the cities of the north became independent states and formed an alliance against the German emperor and the pope. The mercantile cities of Germany also formed strong alliances. The Hanseatic League colonized much of the eastern Baltic coast and monopolized trade in the Baltic until the fifteenth century, bringing wealth to Scandinavia as well as conflict with the Scandinavian kings. Meanwhile, the princes of the smaller German states retained their power and were responsible for electing an emperor dependent upon their support.

The popes of the eleventh to thirteenth centuries unified the western church and encouraged Crusades to win the Holy Land back from the Muslims. Monasteries increased, and in the thirteenth century new religious movements focused on cities and the conquest of the Holy Land, with Franciscans and Dominicans preaching in cities. In the Holy Land, knights dedicated to the protection of Crusaders and Pilgrims formed the orders of the Hospitalers and the Templars, major political forces in the west. Popes opposed emperors, and two, sometimes three different popes were elected, leaving western Christendom without a clear leader. England had unified in the eleventh century under Edward the Confessor, with the Norman Conquest of 1066 tying England to territories in France. In the twelfth and thirteenth centuries conflict broke out several times between England and France for control of these regions. The devastating Hundred Years' War ended in the fifteenth century with France gaining control over most of the territories.

The fourteenth century saw famine and the Black Plague, often seen as divine punishment for the inability of Christianity to unite and control the Holy Land. Jews, who had frequently suffered the wrath of overzealous Christians during the Crusades, were accused of poisoning wells and were banished from parts of Europe.

By the end of the fourteenth century, the borders of the early modern period had been drawn. The new kingdom of Burgundy, incorporating much of the Netherlands, was a center of culture. Northern Italian cities fostered learning and the arts. Monarchs ruled well-defined territories, codifying laws that applied over the entire realm and creating centralized governments. Throughout Europe a renewed interest in classical learning and a humanistic focus in the arts led to the Renaissance, while continued dissent within the Church would lead to the Reformation and religious wars in the north.

Ellen M. Shortell,
Assistant Professor of Art History
Department of Critical Studies
Massachusetts College of Art, Boston

Two thirteenth-century horses and a plow. With the invention of the plowshare and the harness, plowing was made easier, with more crops grown on the same land.

Growth and Prosperity

The Rise of European Commerce and Trade

In the early Middle Ages, harvests were meager and agricultural techniques quite primitive. Tenants who farmed the land used crude lightweight wooden plowshares that simply ripped open the soil without turning it over. Occasionally, they threw manure in the furrows. After that, they simply waited for favorable weather. Any threat to their scant food supply meant immediate famine. They slaughtered most of their cattle every fall because no land produced enough to feed the beasts through the winter.

Even so, by the eleventh century there were signs of a rise in the general standard of living and a population increase. For one thing, a glacial front receded to the north in northern Europe, warming the earth for agriculture. Barren lands, including cut forests and swamps, were claimed for farming, new

settlements were established, and large armies were able to leave for the Crusades.

Important Inventions

Some indications of recovery were already visible in the tenth century. The German emperor Otto I the Great had ended the Magyar threat from Hungary. Viking invasions had become more sporadic. As the general level of safety increased, people could turn to matters other than defense.

Most important among the discoveries that would revolutionize agriculture was that of the curved moldboard that was attached to the plowshare (or blade), perhaps adapted from one used in the eastern provinces of the late Roman Empire. The improved plow not only cut the soil, it turned it over, enabling better crops. An improved harness for draft animals had been imported from central Asia, permitting more efficient use of animal power. Iron horseshoes were introduced. Finally, a system of crop rotation, the three-field system, was developed that left a third of the soil lying fallow (unplanted) at a given time, preventing soil exhaustion. The previous practice had been to leave half the fields fallow at a time. Now, farmers discovered that the soil could recover in a single season after two years of intensive cultivation.

As the use of these innovations spread, there was marked improvement in the food supply. This, in turn, led to improved nutrition, a healthier populace, and lower death rates. In the tenth century, population growth rates in Europe began to increase. Eventually, more cultivated land was needed to feed the burgeoning population. Wilderness areas were taken over for agriculture.

The Economy Starts to Flourish
The tenth-century agricultural innovations caused grain production to increase, but they also had another effect. In the regions where the new techniques were most widely adopted, people were released from basic agricultural production. Many began to develop home industries. This encouraged the rise of a market economy.

Beginning in the eleventh century, industry, too, was marked by technical innovation, particularly in textile production. Most spinning and weaving had taken place in the large manors. Now a pedal loom, perhaps first used in Asia, was introduced in Flanders. It allowed for much faster weaving and significantly greater output. Weavers could produce for market as well as for their own needs. Because of the stepped-up production, the demand for raw wool and spun thread increased, which stimulated the wool trade. The need for marketing outlets, together with the investments required for the new technology, caused the textile industry to become increasingly concentrated in the cities. The newly urbanized industry became an important factor in the rise of commerce in a number of regions, especially in Italy and northwestern Europe.

The Annual Fairs
In the twelfth century, rural annual fairs were held in western Europe to foster contact

Miniature from a twelfth-century manuscript showing a butcher preparing to slaughter a calf

The collecting of blood from a slaughtered pig in preparation for the making of blood sausage

among the merchants and to stimulate business. Traders from north and south needed convenient access to each other. Central location was important and the large cities of the time were not suitable. Flanders was too far north; Lombardy was on the other side of the Alps. Hence, the merchants met on the plains of eastern France, in the county of Champagne. A cycle of large annual fairs was held that began in January at Lagny. On the Tuesday before the middle of Lent, the city of Bar had its turn. Next, the market of Saint Quiriace was held near Provins. In June, the "hot market" (named for the weather) took place at Troyes. In September, there was a second fair in Provins. Later in the fall, the season closed with a "cold market," again at Troyes.

These annual fairs were protected by medieval law. Foreigners who came to trade were exempted from the provisions of local law. The count of Champagne guaranteed the free legal status of the merchants and sent soldiers to enforce his edict. The arrangement, known as the "market peace," was administered by market masters or bailiffs. Ordinarily, there were two of them, a nobleman and a merchant, both appointed by the count. They issued permits to the notaries and the money changers who served the public and appointed a small army of sergeants to maintain order.

These sergeants were sorely needed. Competing merchants and buyers with different customs and languages met at the fairs. Arguments about prices, weights, and

Miniature from
the twelfth-century book
Speculum virginum
(The Harvest of the Grain)

quality of merchandise were bound to erupt. The fairs also had a festival atmosphere. They were not just trade fairs. Magicians performed tricks, singers sang the latest songs, prostitutes did a thriving business, and wine flowed freely. Discipline was strict. Those who broke the rules were sure to fall

The office of a medieval money changer, painted in the first half of the sixteenth century by Marinus Claesz van Roemerswael

into the hands of a sergeant and be dealt swift justice. The market tribunal had to pass judgment between sunrise and sunset, even in the most serious cases, and sentence was executed immediately. The market masters used personal seals (like those used by cities and feudal lords) on all their sentences, a sign of their autonomy.

The annual fairs were a great success. They were eventually organized throughout Europe. Bruges held one; so did Antwerp. Some of these fairs still exist today as carnivals. In the thirteenth century, their commercial aspect began to dwindle, especially for the long-distance trade. Merchants began to conduct their business from offices rather

than in person. If they were rich enough, they sent representatives abroad. Ships had become bigger and better. It was no longer profitable to drag small quantities of merchandise around the country in wagons. New financial practices originating in the fairs made the extensive travel to them unnecessary.

Banks

Many different currencies circulated at the fairs: Venetian coins, French *livres* from Tours, and the British pound sterling. Fairs were flooded with the generally accepted coinage of the city of Provins, minted by the count of Champagne. It was difficult for the layperson to understand the value of the various currencies, especially since considerable amounts of questionable money circulated. Merchants were eager to get their hands on currency that would be accepted at home.

This is where the money changers came in. Sitting behind benches piled with a variety of currencies, they used scales to weigh the coins offered for exchange and kept a small percentage of the amount as a fee. Coins had the same value as the precious metal used to make them. Some changers increased their profits by using false weights, but the penalties were severe. Convicted cheats lost all their possessions. Their benches were broken. *Banco* (bench) *rotto* (broken), the Italians called it, an expression recognizable in the word *bankrupt*.

A great deal of money was always in evidence at the fairs. During the Middle Ages, it was dangerous to travel with bags of gold. The bill of exchange was developed by merchants as a way to avoid the risk. It was used in the following manner: Suppose that merchant A needed to pay merchant B a certain amount of money but did not have the cash. He would have a notary draft a document (an "I owe you" or IOU) in which he promised to pay B the amount in question, on a certain date and at a certain location (for example, at Troyes during the cold market).

This process was taken a step further when merchant A no longer mentioned merchant B by name. A would simply promise to pay the amount at a certain date and location (for instance, the cold market at Troyes) to the bearer of the bill of exchange. If B, however, wanted his money on a different date at a different place, he could sell the bill of exchange. (Perhaps B wanted to cash in his bill of exchange at the Saint Ayoul market because he needed the money quickly, or because he no longer intended to go to Troyes. He might sell the IOU to a colleague

New Monastic Orders: Monks as Peasants

Monasteries became very important in society, beginning in the early Middle Ages. Religious people donated so much land and merchandise to the monastic communities that their simple lifestyle gradually began to resemble that of the wealthy landowners.

This put the monks at odds with the monastic Rule of St. Benedict, which dictated poverty and simplicity. In the eleventh century, some monks and nuns, dissatisfied with what they saw as a violation of spiritual purity, wanted to return to the conditions of the early Christian church. They formed groups which went into the wilderness to begin their own religious orders.

One of these monks was Bruno of Cologne, who founded the small order of the Carthusians at the end of the eleventh century. Carthusian monks lived in groups of twelve, residing in individual huts. Abiding by strict rules of asceticism, they lived in poverty, silence, and solitude. There were only three monastaries, or charterhouses, when St. Bruno died, and the order did not grow popular until the late fourteenth and fifteenth centuries.

The Cistercian order was founded in 1098 by an abbot of a Benedictine monastery named Robert. After an abbey dispute over interpretation of the Rule of St. Benedict, he took some followers to a remote part of France, Citeaux in Burguandy. They reclaimed the wilderness for cultivation and built a successful monastery with its own rules of simplicity. Their concepts appealed to a lot of people. By 1250, there were some 750 Cistercian monasteries across Europe. Suc-

cess itself became a problem and old problems reemerged. To prevent the monasteries from becoming rich, they decided that the only gift the communities could accept was uncultivated land. Furthermore, the monks were required to till the soil themselves.

The monks lived austere lives, but their monasteries produced significant wealth which led to a recurrence of the old socio-religious tensions.

The façade of the abbey of Casmani in Italy, founded by the Cistercians in the twelfth century

who had to be in Troyes, anyway. He would probably do so for a price lower than the face value (the amount stated) of the IOU since the colleague now ran the risk that A might default.)

Money changers were eager to trade in these bills of exchange. They were familiar with financial matters and could make a good profit on them. A full-scale bill-of-exchange market arose. People were prepared to offer prices close to the face value as the day of payment neared. Bills of exchange were often written with long terms, so a creditor could get his money without ever seeing the debtor again. This

had its effect on the annual fairs.

The banking business thrived. A number of money changers moved beyond the well-stocked bench, with its scale, and they began to trade in bills of exchange and to reap profits from coin exchange in the cities. They began to lend money at interest, a practice called usury that was condemned by the Christian church, since it meant profit without work. As a result, the credit industry was conducted exclusively by Jews for a long time. The Christians would eventually modify their view of moneylending, as when one of the popes, in an effort to placate the inhabitants of Lombardy, granted them the right to

Miniature from the twelfth century illustrating a medieval bank. Above are money chests, and clients are entering the office, below.

lend money without it being considered a sin. Sometimes the practice of charging interest was simply overlooked.

The Lombards called themselves "bankers." They became the most important financiers in Europe. Even kings borrowed money from them. At the beginning of the Hundred Years' War, around 1331, the English king Edward III even put up his crown as collateral for loans from Florentine banks. The Lombards had a monopoly on moneylending.

French gold coins from the fourteenth century

Commerce and the Nobility

The nobility continued to live as they had always done. The nobles exploited their vast estates, hunted, and went off to war in the Crusades. Over the course of the next centuries prosperity created by the major inventions of the era was eventually diminished by rising prices.

The Crusaders had tasted the luxury of the East on their journeys through Byzantium and the Muslim territories of the Holy Land. The western aristocracy were received with much pomp by the Byzantine leaders and also made alliances with some of the Arab leaders. Those who were captured by Muslims were brought to their castles. Nobles had stone homes with simple tapestries and fur hangings, while Byzantine luxury was very impressive to visitors, who brought back Oriental arts of war (one of them was an improved siege technique), in addition to Oriental luxury.

The nobles were forced to turn their rustic strongholds into the great castles still evident in Europe today. This was extremely expensive and required a cash flow the nobles did not have. Their wealth was in their landholdings. The only way to obtain cash was through selling their serfs their freedom, which was ultimately insufficient.

The nobles became increasingly short of money. Big cash profits could be made in commerce, but it was carried out in the distant cities and most nobles considered it beneath them to engage in trade. They had to raise the cash from their estates. No longer interested in taxes in kind, they initiated a new kind of lease agreement, replacing the earlier percentage rent with a fixed amount. This frequently went unmodified for centuries, which proved disastrous for their heirs. As money increased in circulation, people raised prices. Inflation became rampant. No one realized that money was being devalued as a result. The fixed contracts made the noble families poorer from generation to generation, and they drifted toward bankruptcy. Emergency measures could only temporarily halt the decay. They could sell land rights to builders or freedom to their serfs only once.

The peasantry benefited most from the nobility's lack of money. The serf-landlord arrangement, once a widespread social institution, gradually evolved into a tenant-landlord relationship that involved some mandatory labor and rent payment that decreased in value with every generation. The peasants who left the countryside for the cities also profited significantly from the poverty of the nobility. It was in the cities that the erosion of the feudal system would manifest itself most clearly in the Middle Ages.

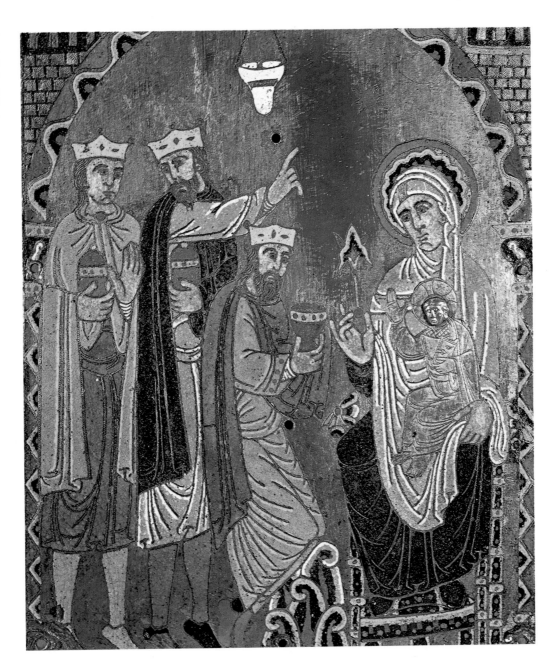

In the twelfth century the French city of Limoges was renowned for its enameled painting. Most popular were religious images, such as this one, depicting the adoration of the Magi.

Towns and Cities

New Systems of Community and Government

In the thirteenth century, Europe was much less fragmented than it had been two hundred years earlier. Powerful rulers had acquired large realms, and cities had formed alliances. Within the expanded realms, princes and lords, independently, were compelled to form alliances and to pledge loyalty to those of higher rank and to the king. The trend toward unity cannot be attributed to deliberate action on the part of the powerful sovereigns of the time, who merely took advantage of the profound social and eco-nomic changes in the twelfth and thirteenth centuries.

Major inventions were followed by a general rise in the level of prosperity, starting at the end of the tenth century. Population increased, trade revived, and money began to play a role. The growing population initially focused on cultivating new land, but eventually countless people left agriculture to build new lives. In the tenth century, merchants already had stopping places where they built more or less permanent homes and some-

The fortified city of Carcassonne (southern France), built c.1150 on the remains of a Muslim castle. The city's defense wall is one mile (1.6 kilometers) long, with fifty-two bastions (projecting parts of the fortification) and only two gates, one of which can be seen in this photograph.

applied. The people who owned the land they lived on were local aristocracy, ruling as landed gentry guided by their own interests, including peaceful dealings with peasants and townspeople. That kind of rule was no longer satisfactory to the new inhabitants. They wanted legislation that reflected the new economic interrelationships. They wanted to know where they stood with regard to troublesome nobles. In short, they wanted their own laws, and they got them. In some instances, landowners gradually made concessions; in others, new laws were enacted. In some places, the landowners themselves established cities, giving them extensive rights in order to attract new people.

These citizen victories over erstwhile authority would never have been possible without some form of organization. Citizens understood early on that they needed to unite, if only to preserve the settlements they established. The wealthiest of them–the merchants–began to meet on a regular basis to discuss the state of affairs in the settlement.

Communes

The term *commune* was used to refer both to the town itself and to its government, as it still is used in several countries in Europe. Another term that was frequently used is *coniuratio* (conspiracy) because the members of the commune would give their meetings a more solid foundation by taking a common oath. Democratic elements were practically nonexistent in the commune movement. Almost everywhere, the rich immediately took exclusive control of the governing body and served only their own interests. We can best illustrate the way a commune was run by taking a closer look at two different cities, Pisa and Rome.

Pisa

Pisa was the first city to play a significant role in the political life of the Middle Ages. Today, the cathedral and the Leaning Tower are reminders of the former glory of its inhabitants. The settlement was situated on the Arno River, close to the sea. A road connected Pisa with the coastal town named Porto Pisano, or the port of Pisa. In the early Middle Ages, the population fit easily within

Villagers are harvesting hay, while in the background the castle of the landlord can be seen.
Miniature from the fifteenth century

times small storerooms. They settled at river entrances, near castles, or outside the old cathedral cities, where some of them made a living providing services to church residences. Some were former peasants grown richer through agriculture or trade, some were merchants, others artisans and masons.

They developed a new type of community where the old laws governing relationships between landowners and tenants no longer

1311

View of the Italian city of Siena, a medieval center that has remained intact up to today. Clearly visible is a network of houses and small alleys, as well as the large central square with the city hall and its belfry.

the city's Roman walls, still standing from the days of Roman dominance.

In the ninth century, a naval base had been established at Pisa to guard against the raids of the Muslims. On one occasion, the Pisans succeeded in conducting a counteroffensive on the African coast. As the Pisans regained control over their own region and Christian culture flourished, Pisa's favorable situation enabled it to develop into an important center. The fact that a Christian fleet was anchored there gave the city an advantage over other settlements. The presence of a bishop in residence made Pisa a religious center. But this was not the end. Arabs conquered Sardinia in 1015, and the Pisans won it back in 1052, with the help of the Genoese.

Throughout the eleventh century, the port and the city continued to grow. By 1100, Pisa had between twelve and fifteen thousand inhabitants, an enormous number for those days. The city was surpassed only by Venice and Rome in all of western Christendom. The number of inhabitants was to double in the twelfth century. Pisa became such an important commercial center that the emperor gave it permission to mint its own coins.

However, by the twelfth century Pisa was no longer the only urban center in the region. Genoa to the north and Florence to the south had become significant rivals. The Pisans were almost constantly at war with the Genoese, while the young city of Florence undermined their position of power inland. Eventually Pisa was put on the defensive. Corsica and Sardinia, once wrested from the Muslims, were conquered by their archenemies. In the late thirteenth century, Pisa gradually turned into a second-class power.

Communal government must have existed as early as the end of the eleventh century in Pisa, judging by a document written by the bishop of Pisa. He mentions "consuls," which helps to establish a time frame for the establishment of communal government. When the commune was officially granted charter in 1142, it already largely controlled the city government. Its powers continued to grow. In 1165, a paid chancellor had to be appointed to serve the council. In that same year, the consuls introduced the use of a town seal. Power, however, remained in the hands of a select group of families that controlled all the offices. The position of consul was unpaid and extremely demanding.

The entire city government revolved around the council of consuls, which had the final word on everything. A forty-member senate was established to function as a kind of advisory board, or auxiliary city council. The actions of the consuls were seldom closely monitored, because the council also appointed the senators. Harsher words were uttered, if at all, in the so-called *parliamentum civitatis* (the city parliament), a meeting of the people where all citizens could air their grievances.

This system did not last very long. Infighting tore the oligarchy (government by the few) apart, while groups lacking any power demanded reforms. In the thirteenth century, the Pisans even brought in a *podesta* (a hired strongman) to govern the city and assure peace among the citizens. By this time, relationships within the urban oligarchies throughout Italy had degenerated to such an extent that city government suffered as a result. The various rulers of Pisa actually did a satisfactory job, gradually diminishing the influence of the council of consuls.

Even so, the typical podesta only concerned himself with the interests of the old oligarchy—in addition, of course, to his own—so that he did not enjoy the trust of the medieval middle class, the merchants and artisans from the guilds. During the second half of the thirteenth century, these guilds controlled Pisa.

Ultimately, all the parties lost. In the fourteenth century, many Italian cities fell into the hands of unscrupulous men who either

Cities depended on their surrounding countryside for their food supply. This French miniature shows merchants bringing their wares to the city marketplaces.

This fourteenth-century fresco by Ambrigio Lorenzetti is an idealized interpretation of city government, free of the feuds and strife that were common in those days

1313

The leaning tower
of Pisa, one of the leading
cities of medieval Italy

When the first cities emerged during the twelfth century, the church encountered new problems. It had never been confronted with so many people crowded together in one place. Out of the cities grew a new religious ideal: the *vita apostolica* (apostolic life).

Under this concept, individuals were to take up what was seen as the life of the early disciples of Jesus, based on simplicity, lack of possessions, and begging for food and shelter while traveling and preaching.

Groups of beggars claiming to be divinely inspired did not correspond with the prevailing customs of the church. Many of the monasteries were quite wealthy and the notion that the church should give all it possessed to the poor was not universally well received. The fact that mendicant (or begging) monks were preaching caused great indignation. Traditionally, only priests were allowed to preach. Many of the itinerant monks were persecuted as heretics.

Around 1200, Francis of Assisi developed a concept more acceptable to the church, because his followers lived in organized monasteries. He was a rich merchant's son who, after having serious illness and several visions, decided that he would dedicate his life to absolute poverty. In the Franciscan monasteries that he founded, Francis decreed that not only individual monks but even monastic communities were not allowed possessions.

One of the reasons the new order fit in well with the cities was the nightly practice of giving all leftover food to the poor, who desperately needed it. The pope approved of the ideas of Francis, finding them unusual but not heretical.

More mendicant orders (for instance, the Dominicans founded by St. Dominic) were established over the next few decades in most European cities.

pushed aside the governing bodies or made them dance to their tune.

Rome

Another example of the troubled development of a commune is the papal city itself. For centuries, Rome had been a bone of contention among local aristocratic families, kings, and holy–or sometimes not so holy–fathers. Aurelian, a section of Rome inhabited by clergy but walled off from the Vatican, was often as chaotic as in the poorly governed Vatican.

Rome had the largest clerical organization of all Christendom, so that it remained a big city, even though its population had been decimated in previous centuries. The countless pilgrims who visited the papal residence

Saint Francis of Assisi (1181–1226), the founder of the monastic order of the Franciscans. Detail of a painting in the Lower Church in Assisi, Italy

put bread on the table for many Romans. Trade revived the Tiber River (which flows through Rome). The population increased substantially, but Rome never became an important commercial center. It remained primarily a city of pilgrims and priests.

In spite of this, widespread popular dissatisfaction with the rule of the pope and the prefect who served as the pope's top official developed. This criticism was expressed in the establishment of a communal govern-

Scene on the back of a fourteenth-century mirror, with four scenes of courteous courtship

ment that the people proudly referred to as their senate, evoking the memory of the ancient senate of the Roman Republic. In the 1140s, this senate was far from being merely a club for gentlemen. That is apparent from the procedure followed by the citizens after a popular uprising in 1144. A city parliament like the one in Pisa chose fifty senators. Forty of these monitored policy, while the ten *ordinarii* (ordinary men) who only held office for six months constituted the actual government. The senators acted with great self-confidence; they even minted coins bearing the ancient abbreviation S.P.Q.R. for *senatus populusque Romanus* (the senate and the people of Rome).

1315

A woman spins wool while attending her swaddled baby in this French miniature from the fourteenth century

Pope Eugenius III (1145–1153) was forced to vacate the city in 1146. He continued to fight the city from the country and was not able to return until 1148. Eventually, the situation became so critical that the senators appointed a *patricius* with almost dictatorial powers to maintain their recently acquired freedom. It was a vain effort. The people lost most of what they had gained. The senate continued but, from then on, the pope appointed all its members.

Agitation continued. Arnold of Brescia, an outstanding preacher and a student of Abelard, appeared in the streets of Rome. He spent five years as a fugitive, unwilling to keep his dangerous opinions to himself. In Brescia, he had made a reputation as an ascetic priest sharply critical of the wealth of the church, demanding that the clergy give up its political role and personal wealth and apply itself to spiritual care: The world, he said, should be left to the lay people. Because the Romans listened, he became a danger to the pope. The Second Lateran Council declared him a heretic, thus making

him an outlaw. He barely managed to escape across the Alps. After spending time traveling through France and the German Empire, Arnold was eventually reconciled with the pope and allowed to resettle in Rome. He had not changed a bit, however, as the pope soon realized. Arnold's sermons about a church independent of worldly rule were received enthusiastically by friends of the old senate.

In 1146, there was another uprising. Arnold promptly joined the rebels. A crowd of two thousand people appointed one hundred senators and two consuls. The senate, full of historical consciousness, elected an emperor. This people's *imperator* (Latin for *emperor*) was a perilous precedent for both the pope and the German emperor. Not only did it directly contradict the pope's claim to the right to crown and control the temporal ruler, it attacked the feudal system. Consequently, the city lost all support from the antipapal nobles. It stood alone. The new pope, Hadrian IV, an energetic Englishman, was not inclined to compromise. He made a pact with German emperor Frederick Barbarossa and put the holy city under a dreaded interdict (effectively, a mass excommunication prohibiting the sacraments, including Christian burial). Both these actions upset the pious population. The closer Barbarossa's troops came, the more support the senate lost. The faithful began to demand that Arnold be sacrificed. Deprived of senate protection, Arnold fell into the hands of Frederick, and he was murdered in 1155.

The history of the Roman commune ends in 1198 with the compromise of Pope Innocent III, by which he acknowledged the prefect and the senate, but with the understanding that the pope would have ultimate control and the prefect would rule according to his wishes. The Romans were apparently satisfied with this system, which functioned satisfactorily for many years.

City and Sovereign

The developments in Rome and in the rest of Italy were by no means representative of the rest of Europe. North of the Alps, things were much calmer. The urban aristocracies did not usually become involved in such extensive struggles, and conflicts between the townspeople and their sovereign did not flare up so violently. In the Holy Roman Empire, some fifty cities succeeded in achieving almost complete independence, but many others maintained close ties with their rulers.

Italy was the foremost developer of city-states. Nowhere else were as many formed as in the region between the Alps and the Tiber. Nowhere else could such metropolises, with such power, be found. The feudal lords could not compete. They settled in the cities or disappeared. Lombardy became a patchwork quilt of small autonomous city-states that dominated and governed the surrounding countryside.

In Flanders and northern France, the other major location of city-states, cities did become a power of the utmost importance, but the count was always strong enough to prevent the division of his land. The citizens of Bruges, Ghent, or Courtrai, for example, however self-reliant they became, probably

In the Middle Ages many large towns gained the privilege of minting currency. This is a French coin that was known as the *franc-à-pied*.

French miniature from the fifteenth century showing the picking of fruit in a rural village near a town situated on a hill in the background

Within the illustration: *Calliopius* · *sce* · *na* · *Theatrum* · *Theatrum* · *Ioculatores*

Spectators gather around a traveling theater group staging a play in a medieval French town. Miniature from the fifteenth century

never really wanted independence. Cities north of the Alps would usually support the central authority.

In the Middle Ages, Italy was far ahead of the rest of Europe in every respect, including urban development. In the German Empire, for instance, Frankfurt, with its nine thousand inhabitants, was considered an enormous city. In Italy, a population of that size was not unusual. Only capitals like London and Paris and economic centers like Ghent and Bruges could actually compare in size and sophistication with the Italian metropolises. Everywhere else, cities remained small. In the early twelfth century the peace was often disturbed because of conflict between the lords. The small cities were unable to defend themselves against the superior strength of their typical enemies. For them, war meant withdrawing behind their ramparts and hoping for a quick end to the conflict. Urban citizens did not aspire to political power. They wanted the safe roads and stability essential to commerce. They

wanted to carry on their lives and their work in peace and quiet. Territorial sovereigns who could provide that peace and quiet found natural allies among them.

Most of the earliest cities had started as settlements which gained the status of city through a series of concessions by landowners. Toward the end of the eleventh century, the rights and obligations defining that status were fairly consistent across northern Europe. First and foremost was the right to make laws within the city. Permission to build walls around the city was also important, as were the governmental regulations that determined the precise extent of the landowner's power. A package of privileges for the urban inhabitants, such as exemption from tolls, was often added. Citizenship was another big question. A city was usually an excellent refuge for runaway serfs. They disappeared in the mass of inhabitants to escape prosecution by their erstwhile lords. Most city dwellers supported them. There was an almost universal rule that whoever had stayed a year and a day in a city was considered free. Some lords actually founded cities and expressly incorporated the year-and-a-day regulation to attract serfs from the estates of their peers. They made especially sure their own serfs were exempt.

The rights of a city were rarely unique. Generally, the landlord granted privileges that were already in effect in other cities. The whole package of rights and regulations making up the city laws was called the city charter. The charter was recognized by the law of the realm, its details beautifully inscribed on parchment. The document was carefully kept in municipal archives. Most European cities today can still produce their original charters.

The Urban Breakdown of Feudalism

Within the city walls, there was no longer any trace of the old feudal pyramid based on the mutual obligations among the landowners, the vassals to whom they granted the land (called fiefdoms), and the serfs who worked it. In the country, relationships remained vertical, landlord authority at the top. In the city, they were horizontal. Everyone was equal, at least in principle. Even the aristocratic families that soon gained control of urban governments were one another's equals. Back in the rural areas, pockets existed, places where feudal society still prevailed.

Guilds

Inside the walls, not all urban citizens concerned themselves with city-wide government. The people living in certain quarters

From the fourteenth century, Flemish towns prospered from the cloth trade. This miniature illustrates the dyeing of cloth in a bath that is kept warm over an oven.

Before the building of public waterworks, fountains were the main water supply for the people in medieval towns. Pollution of these vital sources was punished as a serious offense. Detail from a German painting, c.1476

Musicians playing various instruments in French miniatures from the fourteenth century

practicing a particular craft, they were neither unions of workers nor employers' associations. Merchants and craftsmen in each city organized themselves into professional societies known as guilds. One example is the Paris guild of masons, stonecutters, mortarers, and plasterers, recorded in 1258.

Only guild members were allowed to practice a given craft. The principle of free enterprise did not exist in the Middle Ages in Europe. It did not become solidly established until the nineteenth century. Medieval people took a very different view from the competition-minded business people of today. Fellow craftsmen did not try to dominate the market, to eliminate each other by competition. Instead, they attempted to divide the sales territory fairly, working together. The instrument they used was the guild. Through it, they laid out conditions for the trade. They established the prices of goods and set standards for the quality of the products, the techniques to be used, and the maximum size of the shops. Strict guild masters made sure that the members adhered to the rules.

The guilds functioned as schools for their respective crafts. Anyone wanting to learn a particular trade would apply to a master to be hired as an apprentice. Once acquainted with the rudiments of his craft, the apprentice was promoted to journeyman. With additional experience, he could be made a master, which gave him the right to start his own small business. In the fourteenth century, it was customary for the journeyman to take a kind of exam. He had to produce a "masterpiece" which was judged by the masters of the guild. The guild could thus regulate the size of the trade group. It could keep the number of small businesses in check by allowing only a few journeymen to succeed. It was not uncommon for an excellent craftsman to rise no higher than journeyman, because the masters thought there were enough others already practicing that craft in the city. It was possible for a craftsman to join a guild in another city, but almost everywhere, outsiders were prevented by law from starting their own businesses. This situation continued until the French Revolution put an end to the guild system in most of Europe.

The guilds were also important as social clubs. The guild halls which could be found in every city would often rock with the wild parties of the guildsmen. Guilds vied with one another to have the most impressive processions. They also competed with each other over the chapels they designed for the side walls of the churches. Members congregated in those chapels to worship or attend meetings.

formed their own organizations. Early in the Middle Ages, merchants formed *gigilda* (guilds), clubs that included all their colleagues at a single location. This is the first use of the word, but these clubs were by no means as structured as the later ones of the same name. Sources from the era refer to loose societies which celebrated certain festivities together. In the following centuries, these associations evolved into interest groups for particular trades and became the predominant social institutions called the medieval guilds.

By the eleventh century, all craftsmen were united in guilds. These had taken on a number of roles. Organized by the people

Seal of Richard I the Lionheart (1157–1199). He was a son of Henry II of England and Eleanor of Aquitaine, and married to Berengaria of Navarra.

Rivalry Along the Channel

France and England in the Middle Ages

After the reign of Charles the Bald (823–877) ended with his death, the West Franconia Empire became the weaker kingdom of West Francia. Throughout the tenth century, its kings had done little more than play off their troublesome vassals against each other, a practice which tended to backfire on them. The vassals had demanded more power and more rights in exchange for their dubious support. Whenever a competing royal family appeared, it could always find partisans. Divisiveness became

entrenched. The empire had turned into a chaos of bickering baronies.

The barons, who had no interest in a powerful king, had little trouble in accepting Hugh Capet, a scion of the competing royal family Robertines. His father was Hugh the Great, lord of most of northern France, count of Paris. His mother, Hadewig, was sister of the Holy Roman Emperor Otto I. His sphere of influence in France extended only from Paris to Orléans and, even in this narrow corridor, his power was challenged by rebel-

English miniature from the tenth century depicting King Edgar I (943–975), his hands raised in prayer, standing between the Virgin Mary and Saint Peter. Edgar was the father of King Ethelred the Unready.

Geoffrey V Plantagenet, count of Anjou. He was married to Matilda, the daughter of Henry I of England. His son later became King Henry II of England. This is a funerary plaque of Limoges enamel.

lious powerful members of the West Frankish nobility. For him, the kingship consisted simply of the crown on his head. No power came with it. Unlike the Carolingians, Hugh Capet was fully aware of this fact. He did not attempt to govern outside his own territory.

His successors there followed his example. Inconspicuously, they strengthened their own positions in the domain. It took two cen-

turies for this patience and realism to produce concrete results, but it did so in the reign of King Philip II Augustus who reigned from 1179–1223. Hugh Capet succeeded in effectively expanding his territory across the major portion of the empire where his ancestors had formerly been only one group among the feuding dukes and counts. In his enlarged kingdom, he created a centralized administration which served to reinforce his rule. The muddle of baronies had evolved into a powerful state, and France was now ready to assume a major role.

The eleventh century was essentially similar to the tenth. Anarchy decreased to some extent, because the nobles of this century had greater success in containing their own vassals. No major expansion occurred because each of the barons was too weak. The only power that actually gained in status and influence was the duchy of Normandy.

Normandy was a relatively recent political creation. In 911, Charles the Simple, king of West Francia, had obtained the assistance of an army of Norsemen Vikings from Denmark and Norway in return for a coastal region along the English Channel that became the duchy of Normandy. Part of the agreement was the mass conversion to Christianity of these former assailants. The Norsemen not only accepted the religion of their new home, they soon adopted its customs. In doing so, they lost nothing of their own indomitable energy. It was these Normans (from the Germanic word *Nortmann*) who expelled the Byzantines and Muslims from southern Italy. Since Vikings also controlled the English throne in the early eleventh century, they also set the tone at the Anglo-Saxon court in London.

England

England's liberation from the Norsemen did not last long. After the expulsion of Eric Bloody Axe in 954 and a succession of rulers, power came into the indecisive hands of Ethelred the Unready, who preferred to pay a ransom in gold to prevent further Viking violence. For years, the king paid money (called *Danegeld*) to buy peace for his subjects. Then he abruptly refused to pay further tribute. In order to demonstrate his determination, he organized a large-scale massacre of the Norsemen in his empire. The result, of course, was disastrous. King Sweyn Forkbeard of Denmark launched his entire fleet and ended Ethelred's unpopular realm with little difficulty. Ethelred fled in 1013, and England was once again under Viking control.

King Sweyn, who died in 1014, was succeeded by Canute the Great who united Denmark, England, and Norway. He became king of Denmark in 1014, king of England in 1016, and conquered Norway in 1028. Canute promoted excellent relations with the clergy and thus secured official recognition as a Christian king. During the eight years of his reign, he was undoubtedly the

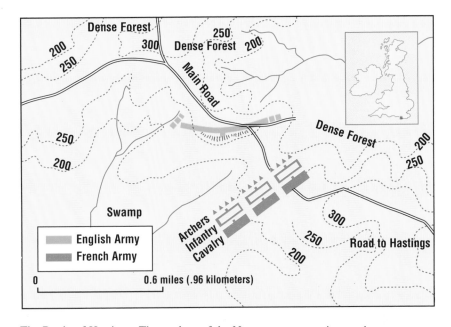

The Battle of Hastings. The nucleus of the Norman army was its cavalry. The English army consisted mainly of footmen armed with axes, swords, and spears, who were unable to ward off a cavalry attack in open terrain. They took a defensive position on top of a steep hill, their flanks covered by woodlands, brooks, and swamps. The Normans did not gain the day until they feigned a retreat, luring the English out into the open, where they were defeated by the cavalry.

Detail of the Bayeux Tapestry showing the English King Harold on the left, as the English are fleeing the battlefield. Below, dead soldiers are being stripped of their armor.

1323

most powerful ruler in the West, other than the emperor himself. Canute died in 1035, leaving his kingdom divided among his three sons. After they reigned for a short time, it disintegrated. England restored the dynasty of Alfred and Ethelred in 1042, and it was back under Anglo-Saxon rule.

The new king, Edward, son of Ethelred the Unready, was so remarkable for his piety he is known to history as the Confessor, and this is the category–pious, but not martyred –under which the Church declared him a saint in 1161. He seems to have had little administrative talent. The young king had spent the difficult period after Sweyn's invasion in Normandy and this left its traces. At his London court, Norman nobles predominated, because Edward trusted them. This was perhaps justifiable. The English lords were unreliable and rebellious and Edward could barely prevail against them. The country was dominated by powerful men, like Count Godwin and his successor, Harold, who each served the king as a kind of prime minister. They used Edward to legitimize their own powers.

An additional problem arose. Since Edward was unable to produce children, his throne would be vacant after he died. There was, however, a surfeit of candidates for it. King Harald Hardrada of Norway claimed the right of succession; Duke William in Normandy pointed to a vague promise made by Edward; and the powerful Count Harold was at the English court. It was determined that William had the most reasonable claim. He succeeded by accident in obtaining the allegiance of his competitor Harold.

Oath or no oath?

One day in 1064 Harold was sailing on the English Channel, probably on a diplomatic mission, when a strong wind drove him toward the continent of Europe. He was arrested and taken to the Norman court of Duke William of Normandy where he was received with much hospitality. Harold swore an oath, interpreted variously by the few available sources. The Normans claimed that Harold had given a pledge of allegiance to the Duke and was therefore obliged to support William's claims to the English throne. The followers of Harold denied this. It was not clear how William could have pushed his rival to the point of swearing allegiance.

Following the oath, Harold spent some time at William's court. The two organized a well-planned campaign against the Duke of Brittany, enemy of both Normans and English. After it was over, Harold traveled back to London, where his position had apparently not suffered during his absence.

Coin portraying William the Conqueror

Detail of the Bayeux Tapestry, showing Norman soldiers carrying arms and armor to be loaded onto ships for the invasion of England

Hastings

In 1066, the pious Edward died. It is thought that he named Harold as his successor, and he was crowned as Harold II the day after Edward died. The English people were happy to gather around his throne but the other pretenders refused to accept him. When Harold showed no signs of being intimidated by them, they mounted separate expeditions to England.

Initially, fortune did not side with William of Normandy. A head wind kept the duke's fleet in Norman ports, while the Norse *drakkars* (Norman/Viking boats) rapidly crossed over to the coast near York. An army of local English lords was waiting for them. The Norsemen had little trouble breaking through them. In the meantime, Harold had feverishly mobilized his people's militia. He hurried northward with the house carls (commoners who served aristocrats), his bodyguard, and elite troops. Five days after

their first victory, on September 28, the Norsemen met the Anglo-Saxon army at Stamford Bridge. The Viking Harald Hardrada was overwhelmingly defeated. Harold's crown was safe for the moment.

Then the wind changed. It filled the sails of William's ships and the Normans crossed the channel. They landed on the English coast near Hastings. Harold's army was slowed down and weakened by battles with local populations as they traveled south. An exhausted army arrived at Hastings. The Normans had formed a battle line on a hill. The terrible battle that ensued almost ended in a victory for Harold, but the people's militia and the house carls broke through the Norman lines. The militia, widely dispersed, immediately started a disorganized attack. This gave the much more experienced Normans the chance to massacre them. On October 14, when only the worn-out house carls were left, the Normans attacked the

The medieval castle of Dover, England's leading port after 1066. Together with four other ports along the Channel, it maintained the English fleet in exchange for freedom from taxes.

Henry II and Thomas Becket

The conflict between Henry II and Thomas Becket is one of the most dramatic episodes in the struggle for power between secular rulers and the church. When Henry II became king of England in 1154, central authority was almost nonexistent. Henry was determined to recover royal authority. In his attempts to reestablish his power, he found a supporter in Thomas Becket, the head of his chancery (the high court responsible for civil matters).

The king was much more of a warrior than an administrator. He sought the insight of Thomas Becket. In 1162, the king made him archbishop of Canterbury, thinking that in so doing he would get an important supporter in the English church. This proved to be a fatal miscalculation. In the same determined and convinced fashion with which he had once worked for the king, Thomas Becket now began to serve the interests of the church. The former friends became bitter enemies.

Their most intense conflict erupted over the English system of jurisdiction. Henry sought to get absolute control over church as well as state jurisdiction. In the Clarendon Constitution, he recorded that clerics (who were usually tried only by the church) had to be tried instead by royal authorities. Appeal to the pope, he said, would only be possible with royal consent.

Becket could not accept this. Forced to flee to France, he continued to write pamphlets in opposition to Henry's activities. The pope, who in principle agreed with Becket, did not wish to enter into a conflict with the king. He succeeded in coming to an agreement with Henry in 1170, and Becket returned to Canterbury.

New conflict soon erupted. When Henry asked the bishop of York to crown his son (something usually done by the bishop of Canterbury), Thomas Becket sent him one of many angry letters. This annoyed Henry, who wondered aloud if nobody could free him of this irritating churchman. Some of his vassals took this literally. They killed Thomas Becket in his own church in front of the altar.

There were repercussions throughout Europe. The murder caused a wave of indignation. The king of France condemned the assassination. The pope proclaimed Becket a

martyr and made him a saint in 1173. Henry was totally politically isolated, and that same year he was forced to publicly condemn the execution and made to visit the grave as a penitent. He had to recall the Clarendon Constitution.

Thomas Becket became one of the most popular saints of the Middle Ages, his grave visited by pilgrims every year. Two centuries after his death, the English author Geoffrey

Miniature from the thirteenth century depicting the murder of Thomas Becket in the Cathedral of Canterbury

Chaucer would write his book *The Canterbury Tales* about a fictional group of these pilgrims.

elite troops and picked them off one by one. That night, Harold lay dead on the battlefield among his loyal followers. William had conquered his kingdom. He was crowned in Westminster Abbey on December 25.

The two invasions in 1066 had taken only three weeks, but they would change England forever. Within a few years, the final resistance of the Anglo-Saxons would be broken. In the meantime, William had begun to reward his fighters with land. He created some two hundred fiefs and gave them out to his fortunate vassals. They, in turn, divided the fiefdoms among their own aides, giving England a new feudal nobility. William made sure that he doled out land, not power, by keeping the two hundred fiefs small and isolated, separated by his own royal preserves. He retained the useful parts of the Anglo-Saxon administrative system–taxes, for example.

William the Conqueror became the most powerful monarch of Europe within his own domain. He exploited the native Anglo-Saxons for the benefit of the Normans. It would take more than a century for the original people and their new lords to adjust to each other and merge into a national culture. Anglo-Saxon speech was radically altered by the Norman French, becoming the English language.

After the death of William the Conqueror in 1087, his carefully constructed system came near to collapse. His sons, Rufus, Robert, and Henry, fought one another, fomenting a series of rebellions between 1130 and 1150. William's dynasty died out, but the bloody interim created by his sons seriously weakened royal authority.

In 1150, the crown went to Henry Plantagenet, Duke of Anjou, through one of William's daughters, Matilda. Because Henry had acquired Normandy by inheritance and extensive areas in France by marriage to Eleanor of Aquitaine, he could mobilize sizable power to restore the position of the English crown. In a series of campaigns, he brought the rebellious noblemen back in line. He subsequently reformed royal administration so that it would continue to function during his absence in France. He gave primary responsibility for all state documents to the chancellor, who became the chief administrator of the kingdom. He restored and strengthened the office of the exchequer which administered the country's finances. Henry's most impressive accomplishments were in the field of jurisprudence. He simplified legal proceedings. He created a central court, presided over by the king himself. He also introduced traveling justices (justices in *eyre*) who held court in the provinces and moni-

tored the local administrators.

During his reign, it became evident that the kingdom of England was no longer totally independent. It was becoming increasingly involved in European affairs. Europe, therefore, had to reckon more seriously with the English king.

Toughness in Paris

While the French kings had been forced to watch Duke William, their vassal, make himself a triumphant career in England, they could do nothing about it. They had to focus mainly on their own estates. After Hugh Capet, a remarkable series of competent, long-reigning kings ascended the throne. They restored power in their fiefs and retained the right to make all appointments with regard to church affairs. Their prestige increased steadily.

In 1137, Louis VII ascended the throne. In some aspects, he resembled Edward the Confessor, both in piety and in general incompetence. Fortunately, a host of able people were at his service. They succeeded

Miniature from the *Chronicles of France*, depicting Louis VI (1018–1137) capturing Orléans. He succeeded in bringing peace and in expanding the power of the royal family.

Seal of Philip II Augustus, brother of Richard I the Lionheart and John Lackland

Miniature from the
Chronicle by Villani, depicting
Philip II Augustus in the
battle of Bouvines

in making their king the most powerful ruler of France by arranging a marriage with Eleanor, the duchess of Aquitaine. Aquitaine was by far the largest fief of the French crown. The marriage gave Louis approximately a third of his official kingdom.

The fact that it ended in disaster was not the fault of the advisers, but of the spouses: Eleanor and Louis hated each other almost from the start. King Louis was dull and sheepish, while Eleanor was definitely spirited. After fifteen miserable years, Louis wanted to divorce his wife. He was more than willing to exchange Aquitaine for his happiness. The marriage was annulled, allegedly because Eleanor had not given the king any sons, but only two daughters. (The official reason given for that was the close genetic relationship said to exist between Eleanor and Louis.)

Eleanor was furious about the humiliation she had suffered. She married again almost immediately in 1152, this time to Henry Plantagenet, the duke of Anjou, two years

before he became king of England. He had already succeeded to the duchy of Normandy. With the addition of Eleanor's fief, Henry became by far the most powerful man in France.

The only thing Louis could do was to conspire with his remaining vassals against Henry. He had reasonable prospects of success. Henry did not rule a kingdom but a union of personal interests, a series of very different regions which happened to have the same lord. All his life, Henry had to face constant resistance and rebellion in his territories. Only in England was he able to build a durable system of government, but in Henry's eyes, England was a backwater: He was a French baron with French interests, all located on the continent.

In 1180, the aged Louis was succeeded by his fifteen-year-old son, Philip Augustus. The new king was weak and sickly. He did not cut an impressive figure and showed remarkably little interest in battles and military victory. He was, however, a sly diplomat

with a talent for intrigue. This became evident during the first years of his reign. Marriage to Isabelle of Hainault, a Flemish noblewoman, brought him the duchy of Artois in northern France. By winning a war with local princes, he also gained power over Vermandois, so that Eleanor had to swear loyalty to him, as countess of Vermandois.

At the same time, disorder broke out in the lands of the aging Henry Plantagenet. His sons, Henry, Richard the Lionhearted, King John I, and Geoffrey, were fighting over their inheritance. The father made matters worse by supporting his youngest son, John Lackland. Philip Augustus used intrigue wherever he could to fan the fire, ultimately supporting John and his brother, Richard, in a conspiracy against their father. The old king was defeated, but removed a knotty problem for his sons by dying shortly afterward. When the king was succeeded by his oldest son, Richard, Philip Augustus knew that the younger one, John Lackland, was unhappy. Philip helped John behind the scenes. This resulted in a protracted war between Richard and Philip, in which John Lackland (who was later to sign the Magna Carta) played a devious role.

In 1199, Richard died during a siege. John Lackland succeeded him, forcing Philip Augustus to look for yet another contender to the throne to further his own interests. He chose Geoffrey, third son of Henry and Eleanor, the Duke of Brittany. War continued, now between John and Philip. John was slowly put on the defensive by Philip's military and diplomatic actions. After years of

On his way home from the Third Crusade, Richard I the Lionheart was captured and held prisoner by Emperor Henry VI of Germany. After Richard swore an oath of loyalty and promised to pay ransom, he was set free and returned to England. Miniature from the thirteenth century

Relief from the twelfth century depicting soldiers of the infantry of a medieval army

Statue of the German emperor Otto III, who was raised at the court of his uncle, Richard I the Lionheart

fighting, John was forced back to the duchy of Gascony in southern France. Here there were enough economic ties to England to make the people want to remain under the Plantagenets. All of Henry's other territories had fallen to Philip.

Philip was increasingly able to position himself as the king of all French territory. He was able to turn the feudal system (which had previously taken so much power from royalty) to his advantage. This was particularly true in the case of John Lackland. John

A man warms his feet and dries his boots near a fire in a miniature used as illustration for the psalms of February, from a thirteenth-century English manuscript

had married a noblewoman already promised to another man, the count of LaMarche, who was entitled to a generous payment as a rejected fiance. The count appealed to the French king in Paris. Philip Augustus summoned John, who was formally still his vassal, to appear before the vassal court. As he had expected, John refused to appear. Philip, as his lord, could therefore declare John's fiefs annulled. In practice, he had to execute this declaration by military force, but the principle of the king as supreme lord was confirmed.

The Battle of Bouvines
The French king became embroiled in other conflicts. At the time, the German Empire was being torn apart by a civil war between pretenders to the throne. They were supported either by John or by Philip. In 1214, John Lackland and the German emperor, Otto IV, decided to mount a joint attack on their mutual enemy. Suddenly, the French king was threatened from both East and West. He decided to deal with the German enemy first, hoping that John Lackland—as was his custom—would not move too quickly.

Only eight hundred knights were left to guard the western border, while the French main force awaited the entrance of Emperor Otto's army in France. Near the town of Bouvines, the battle erupted. Otto suffered serious defeat. Probably to his own surprise, Philip Augustus had halved the power of his enemies. In Paris, the people celebrated for days. Amid cheering crowds, the king made his entry into the city. His throne and his kingdom were saved. John Lackland was obliged to resign himself to the loss of most of his French fiefs. He retained only Gascony in the Southwest.

His military successes enabled Philip Augustus to strengthen his administrative grip on the kingdom. In doing so, he deliberately moved outside the feudal structures and created a new function, the stewardship (*bailliage*). The steward (*bailli*) was not a vassal, but an official who received a salary instead of a fief. He administered a district of the kingdom according to directives from Paris. He was required to report annually to Paris, and he could be transferred. The steward was completely dependent on an influential king for his income and position. Thus, Philip Augustus created an administrative apparatus which had an interest in being loyal to the monarchy.

By 1200, kingdoms had been created in France and England where the rulers had acquired similar power by quite different means. In England, William's conquest had converted the prefeudal kingdom in one blow into an absolute monarchy, albeit one where the sovereign pulled as many feudal strings as possible. His position reinforced his hold on the most useful administrative elements of Anglo-Saxon royal power. In France, the development of absolute monarchy was more gradual. The Capets remained in the background for generations, paying minimal attention to the kingdom as a whole, as they strengthened their grip on their own territory. During the twelfth century, they were able to expand their domain in bits and pieces, improving their position with respect to their vassals. During the feudal struggle with their most powerful vassal, Henry Plantagenet, they established undisputed royal authority. Once this was accomplished, they undertook development of an administrative system independent of their vassals, utilizing officials in their own employ. Of interest here is the fact that feudal values were both used and undermined at the same time.

Frederick I Barbarossa wearing a crusader's outfit. He led the Third Crusade in order to drive Saladin from Palestine, but drowned on his way to the Holy Land. Here he is shown receiving a copy of a history of the First Crusade (as inspiration) from the provost of the monastery of Schäftlarn.

Popes and Emperors

The Universal Powers in the Twelfth Century

German emperor Henry V died in 1125, leaving no heirs. The rulers of Germany's several principalities and duchies, along with important bishops, became "electors," each of whom had a vote in selecting the new emperor. The search resulted in civil war. The nobles were divided about the kind of emperor they wanted in power. One group advocated a strong emperor who would base his power on the Church. They chose Conrad of the House of Hohenstaufen. The other group was a coalition of reformers in the style of Cardinal Hildebrand, Pope Gregory VII, who did not want emperors appointing bishops, and vassals interested in furthering their own autonomy. This group opted for a less influential ruler, Lothar, from the Welf family. Lothar was elected king and in 1133 was crowned Emperor Lothar III by Pope Innocent II.

This rivalry over imperial succession was the start of years of dynastic feuding. Hohenstaufen supporters were called Waiblingen, after a favorite residence of their candidates. The other party called itself the Welfs. The battle was also waged in Italy. There the names were Guelphs and Ghibellines, more commonly used in English.

After twenty-seven years of confusion, it

Italian miniature
from the twelfth century
depicting Frederick Barbarossa
entering the city of Milan
with his troops

seemed that the time for a compromise had
come. The most important rulers of
Germany, religious as well as laypeople,
supported Frederick of Hohenstaufen, nicknamed Barbarossa (*barba* for beard; *rossa*
for red) because of his red beard. His mother
was a Welf. Frederick's candidacy was generally accepted and he seemed to embody the
perfect compromise. He named the most
important Welf, Henry the Lion, duke of
Saxony, in his will and gave him Bavaria, in
addition. Frederick faced the almost impossible task of restoring the authority of the
emperor. The traditional authority of the
monarch had been eroded by the outcome of
the controversy over investiture, the right to
appoint church officials. This was the issue
that had concerned Pope Gregory, specifical-

Italy in the
twelfth century

ly the practice of having lay royalty "invest" bishops, giving them the ring and staff that were the symbols of their office. Since bishops often held secular positions as well, which made them vassals of the king, lay investiture seemed reasonable under feudalism. At the Concordat at Worms in 1122, the Church was given the right to elect and invest new bishops, but in the presence of the emperor. He was to confer any property of the bishopric to the new bishop using a non-religious symbol, the scepter. The resolution at Worms enhanced the administrative authority of the clerics, just as it undermined Frederick's.

The new emperor had an additional problem. The largest part of his realm had been granted in fief in order to secure supporters during the fight over the succession to the throne and the war that followed it. The royal vassals who had been granted fiefdoms had given them, in turn, to lower nobility who arranged for serfs to work the land. This began the feudalization of the German Empire. In this feudal system, the dukes occupied controlling positions, not the emperor. The dukes were members of high nobility who controlled a duchy. Some had more local power than the emperor.

In the Italian part of the empire, imperial authority was challenged by the great cities that had developed. Merchant aristocracies had assumed the control once held by both resident bishops and the emperor.

Frederick, required to maintain the fragile compromise in Germany, turned his attention to Italy, probably reasoning that an Italian adventure might divert attention. As happened so often in the past, the state of affairs in Rome provided justification.

Many Romans at the time did not accept the political sovereignty of the pope. They had established a council of citizens, called the commune, to which even the pope was required to submit. Several popes were forced into exile for refusing to acknowledge its authority. Street fights over the issue were a regular occurrence. The pope at that time, Hadrian IV (1154–1159), shared the fate of many of his predecessors. He recognized that he and Frederick had similar interests, such as controlling the north Italian cities and suppressing the communal movement.

The emperor crossed the Alps in 1154–1155 with his army and quickly defeated the forces of their common enemy. Frederick met with the pope in Rome. The custom of the time was that the ruler of the Roman Empire should hold the pope's stirrup as a sign of homage to him when he wished to dismount. For Frederick, the gesture was unacceptable. He hesitated as the

pope waited arrogantly for his help. Directly requested to hold the stirrup, he did so but said in an audible voice, "For Petrus, not for Hadrian."

Another incident took place two years later. A papal letter arrived during an important meeting of the Diet (German parliament) in Besançon, at the time under

Miniature from the *Chronicle of the Guelphs* showing Frederick I Barbarossa on his throne. To his right stands his son and successor, Henry VI, and to the left his youngest son, Frederick.

The remains of the imperial palace in Gelnhausen, Germany, built by Frederick I Barbarossa on an island in the River Kinzig

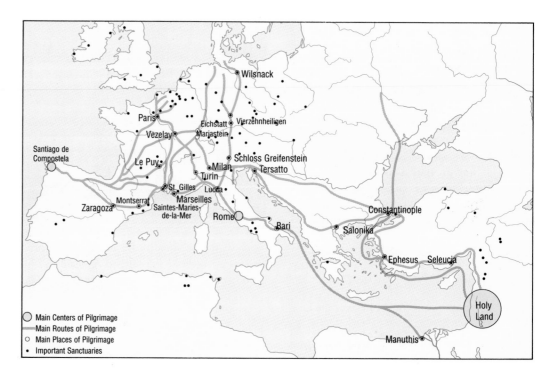

Medieval
Pilgrimage Routes
in Europe

○ Main Centers of Pilgrimage
— Main Routes of Pilgrimage
○ Main Places of Pilgrimage
• Important Sanctuaries

Wilsnack
Paris
Eichstatt   Vierzehnheiligen
Vezelay   Mariastein
Santiago de
Compostela
Le Puy   Schloss Greifenstein
Milan   Tersatto
Turin
St. Gilles
Lucca
Montserrat   Marseilles
Zaragoza   Saintes-Maries-   Rome
de-la-Mer   Bari
Constantinople
Salonika
Ephesus   Seleucia
Holy
Land
Manuthis

German control. Translated for the German nobles by the reformist Cardinal Roland, a sentence read, "It would have pleased the pope if, in addition to the emperor's crown, Your Excellency had also received from our hands even larger *beneficia*."

The word *beneficium* had two connotations. Originally, it meant benediction, or blessing, but in official documents, it was used to mean fiefdom. The implication of papal authority over imperial was clear. The Diet was furious and Roland was nearly stoned. Frederick Barbarossa declared that he did not take his power from the pope but only "from God."

The Emperor Demands His Rights

A year after the incident in Besançon, the emperor crossed the Alps again to set things straight in Italy. During a Diet session in Roncaglia, he demanded the return of all royal prerogatives. These included the royal privileges of collecting tolls and taxes and minting coins, governmental matters that had long before fallen into the hands of local rulers. Frederick sent *podestas* (hired strong men or rulers) to every city in Italy.

It was a gamble. The Italian cities united against the podestas. Frederick was suddenly faced with a dangerous rebellion. The emperor concentrated on Milan, the center of the rebellion. He defeated the rebels there in three years, leveling the city in the process and driving out the inhabitants. The fate of Milan was enough to make other cities act more cautiously. In the meantime, however, Pope Hadrian had died and the assembled prelates chose the German Cardinal Roland as successor. As Pope Alexander III (1159–1181), he became Frederick Barbarossa's most dangerous opponent. With the emperor's support, the minority group in the papal elections held a council to appoint an antipope. Despite the fact that the antipope was only recognized in the areas under Frederick's control, the new pope was forced to vacate the papacy in Rome. He fled to France. It became apparent during these developments that Frederick's earlier victory in Italy was far from definitive. A union of cities opposed to his authority, actively supported by the pope, was formed in Lombardy. These rebels even

Effigy of Henry the Lion on his tomb in Brunswick, Germany. Henry was banished to England for three years by Frederick I Barbarossa.

founded a new city, Alessandria. Frederick could undertake no new action in Italy for a full six years after this union, the Lombard League, was created in 1167. Two years after the invasion of Italy, it assembled Italian forces and defeated the emperor at the Battle of Legnano in 1174. The victory was to have major impact.

Frederick was forced to change his view

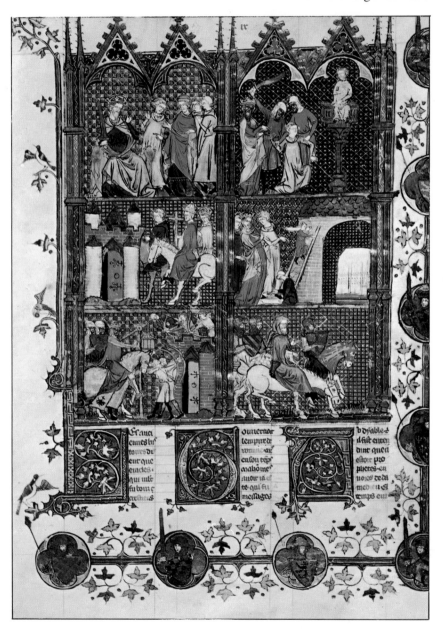

Page from a book about the life of Godfrey of Bouillon. It shows several scenes from the conquest of Jerusalem by the Muslim army of Saladin

on the pope. Alexander took a moderate position. The antipope had to step aside and Alexander III be recognized as pope, but Frederick could keep his sovereignty over the German church. That ended the grand alliance between the pope and the Lombard League. Frederick concluded a peace with the league, based on a compromise. He ceded most of his royal rights in the cities in exchange for the recognition of his authority by the urban magistrates. New appointments would be subject to his confirmation.

The Fall of the Lion

After exhausting Italy's possibilities, Frederick turned to the German part of the empire. The nobles watched with anxiety as he tried to minimize his dependency on them, modifying the feudal system they had long dominated.

By the eleventh century, common people known as *ministeriales* could go fairly far at the imperial court as civil servants. Barbarossa made them the foundation of his rule. He also bound the lower nobles to him by handing out choice positions at court, which they preferred to tending their small estates in the country. The Church, too, felt Frederick's touch. Worms or no Worms, he kept control over appointments.

His methods ran counter to the Guelph conception of imperial rule. The most powerful Guelph, Henry the Lion, wanted the crown himself. He had refused to participate in the Italian campaign. After the defeat at Legnano, he openly objected to Frederick.

The emperor realized that he had to settle with Henry. Complaints from the Lion's fiefdoms provided the rationale for Frederick to call him to the royal court of justice, but the Saxon duke refused to appear. Using arguments from regional, feudal, and even Roman law, the emperor ousted Henry. He divided the duke's vast lands among his own supporters. As a result, Frederick's status and power increased dramatically.

Italy had not slipped his mind. There, too, he was successful. Frederick arranged for a marriage between his eldest son, Emperor Henry IV, and Constance, the heiress of the Norman kingdom of Sicily. With this union, the powerful nation, once his sworn enemy and a devoted supporter of the pope, came into Hohenstaufen hands.

Pope Clement III found himself in a bind. In 1189, when all of Western Europe prepared for the Third Crusade, the only leader he could call on for support was the undisputed emperor of the West. Frederick Barbarossa had no chance to make himself immortal, as the Crusaders were promised. He drowned in a river on his way to southern Turkey in 1190.

Barbarossa became a legend in the Germany of the sixteenth to eighteenth centuries. He sleeps in a mountain, they said, and if you put your ear to a certain stone you can hear his beard grow. He would only awake when Germany was in great danger, they said.

After his death in 1190, the Hohenstaufen triumphs continued. His son Henry VI inherited solid recognition, not only in Germany but throughout the rest of Italy. He controlled

The Fourth Crusade

One of the greatest ambitions that Pope Innocent III had was to recapture Jerusalem from the Muslims. Saladin had conquered the city in 1187, killing many of the Christian inhabitants, and seizing the rest of the Crusaders' territory, as well. The situation had not changed despite the Third Crusade.

Pope Innocent III raised a new army of Crusaders in 1202. This time the plan was to leave from Venice, reaching the Holy Land by ship, but departure was delayed while the organizers sought sponsors. The Venetian merchants finally acquiesced.

The Crusaders then set out for Constantinople. Where Goths, Persians, Bulgarians, and Arabs had failed, this expedition turned out to be a success. Constantinople was captured, burned, and plundered by the Crusaders. Emperor Alexius IV was soon murdered by Murzuphlus, who had himself crowned Emperor Alexius V. The Crusaders reassembled and attacked Constantinople a second time, replacing Alexius V with one of their own leaders, Baldwin, the count of Flanders.

As the victor, Venice received a large number of trading posts. Hundreds of noble Crusaders were made into the emperor's vassals, although they often had yet to conquer the lands that they would hold. The rest of the army went back home, loaded with gold, works of art, and precious manuscripts. The Fourth Crusade never reached Jerusalem, and Innocent's dream of making it a Christian city was never realized.

The Latin empire of Constantinople survived for some sixty years after that, but its existence was tenuous. The vassals fought each other and their emperor, the native inhabitants were hostile toward the conquerors, and, in a few parts of the empire like Nicaea and Trebizonde, the Greek sovereigns managed to continue their rule. In 1261, Michael Paleologus, king of Nicaea, managed to reconquer Constantinople when the citizens opened the gates of the city for him.

The Crusaders' siege of Constantinople in 1204, depicted in a fifteenth-century miniature

name: bete dar ich dich cigelich en sehe.

Illustration from a fourteenth-century manuscript showing the ceremony of investiture: The emperor hands the marks of honor to a nobleman, thus giving him the right to borrow land

Innocent III, pope from 1198 to 1216

the Norman kingdom of Sicily, the best organized state in Christendom.

However, this very success led to an almost automatic reaction by that other universal power, the pope. Blocked by the emperor at every turn, he saw the traditional papal support of the Normans disappear and his own position in the Papal States threatened. Yet twenty years after Frederick Barbarossa's death, the papacy would be at the pinnacle of its power, with Innocent III (1198–1216).

Dominium mundi

The investiture controversy had caused many people to think about the position of the Church within the political system. If the pope was indeed the earthly representative of Christ, they asked, how could he have superiors? Even the emperor had to be considered below him, a position implicit in the fact that the Holy Roman Emperor received his crown from the hands of the pope. The pope, in this view, possessed *dominium mundi* (sovereignty over the world), supervisory responsibility for the actions of secular rulers.

In reality, there was little to substantiate this claim in the first half of the twelfth century. Popes were not allowed to govern their own city, let alone achieve a *dominium mundi*. The papacy only gained prominence when the pope needed allies against the overbearing Frederick Barbarossa. The emperor had countered by bringing the erstwhile papal-dominating Norman kingdom into his sphere of influence by marital arrangement. The roles appeared to have been reversed again. Frederick's son and successor, Henry VI, was a bold man who did not look kindly on half measures. He achieved his goals with rampant violence; his wars in Lombardy also yielded an important part of the Papal States. Although he had been crowned king of Sicily, he had to wage war to actually take the throne, which he did in 1194. He then attacked the Lombard cities ruthlessly. He frequently spoke of his ambition to dominate the world.

When Henry VI died in 1197, his son Frederick II was only a child. The Norman nobles didn't want Henry's descendant to succeed him, and refused to cooperate with his widow. Henry's sudden death gave them the opportunity to reduce the power of the Norman throne. The oppressed Guelphs seized their chance to set up a new emperor. They chose Otto IV of Brunswick in Germany, the son of Henry the Lion. A fierce war broke out between his supporters and those of the Hohenstaufen candidate, Henry's younger brother, Philip of Swabia.

Miniature from the fourteenth century showing a medieval banquet, with servants carving and carrying, and musicians playing their instruments. Host and guests wear the Order of the Golden Fleece.

Fresco attributed to Giotto in the upper church in Assisi, depicting Pope Innocent III having the famous dream where St. Francis supports the church that is on the verge of collapsing

1341

Relief from the twelfth century above the door of the cathedral in Angoulême (France): two fighting knights on horseback, armored in long mail tunics.
The knight on the left succeeds in forcing his opponent from the saddle with his lance.

Pope Innocent III

Innocent III had ascended the papal throne in 1198. While attention was focused on war between the Guelphs and the Hohenstaufens, Innocent resolved problems in Rome. He reconciled his differences with the old enemy of papal authority, the city council of Rome, by withdrawing altogether from city government. After the reconciliation, the pope directed his attention to the rest of the country. He subjugated the troublesome nobles of the Papal States with cold-blooded violence. His authority now stretched from Rome north to Ancona, on the Adriatic Sea.

With nothing to fear at home, Innocent went farther afield. He supported the Guelph Otto IV against the Hohenstaufen Philip of Swabia for the Norman throne, in return for Otto's agreement to give up all attempts to influence church appointments.

However, in the south, he supported the Hohenstaufens against the Sicilian nobles. He assisted the widow of Henry VI, in getting her three-year-old son recognized as heir to that throne. The price was high: The sovereignty that Norman rulers had always enjoyed over the Church passed into the hands of the pope. Henry's widow had to swear fealty to Innocent. She also appointed him as guardian of little Frederick.

Part of the text of the Magna Carta, the basis of the English constitution signed by John Lackland in 1215 after pressure from the nobility and the clergy

Otto IV proved to be an untrustworthy ally. After his coronation as emperor in 1209, he began meddling in church appointments. Innocent was forced to excommunicate him in 1210, along with his followers. Innocent now proposed to place his ward Frederick on the throne. Together with the king of France, Philip Augustus, Innocent started burrowing among Otto's supporters–one of the reasons for Otto's western expedition which had taken such a disastrous turn on the battlefield of Bouvines. That sealed his fate. The Guelph party dissolved and Frederick was generally recognized as emperor. Again, major concessions were demanded and had to be met. Frederick not only had to repeat all of Otto's promises but he also had to swear that he would never unite Sicily with the Holy Roman Empire.

Interdict

The Hohenstaufens were not the only ones subject to the pope's interference. King Philip Augustus brought on the papal penalty called an interdict. This excluded him from certain church offices, sacraments, or privileges. To believers in the Middle Ages, interdiction was a severe punishment, barring the path to salvation.

The pope declared it against Philip Augustus because of his treatment of his second wife. After the death of his first wife, Isabella of Hainault, in 1189, the French king had decided to marry a Danish princess, Ingeborg, who could provide an alliance with the king of Denmark, Canute VI, still a relatively important power. The marriage was performed with great ceremony. After the festivities, bride and groom retired for their wedding night. The next morning Philip Augustus banned his wife from the palace. The reason has always been a great mystery. She went to a convent where she would spend the next twenty years. Philip

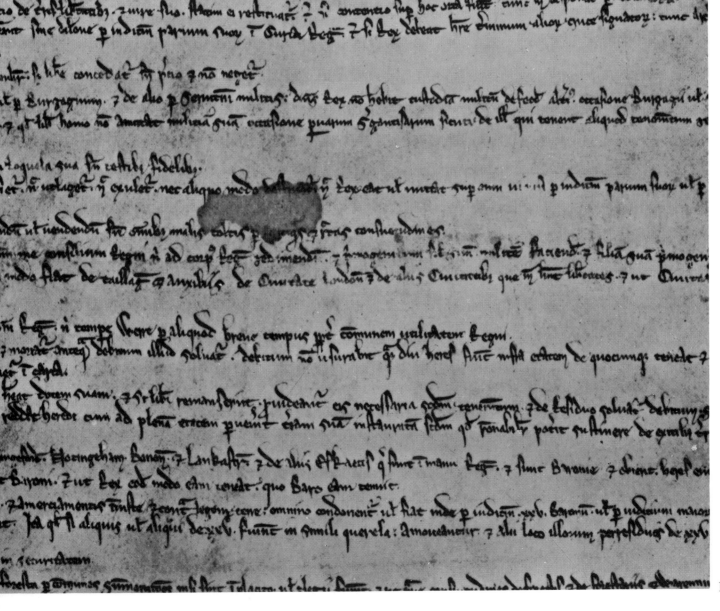

had the marriage annulled through a council of bishops, the final insult. His wife would not stand for that abuse. She appealed to the pope, who decided in her favor. When Philip Augustus persisted in his refusal to take her back, the pope proclaimed the interdict.

The interdict was not obeyed in most of Philip's empire. Guided by high prelates, religious life continued as usual. Philip took another wife, Agnes of Meran in 1196, who bore him two children. The marriage was not recognized by the pope. After her death in 1201, a compromise was reached. Philip Augustus took Ingeborg back in 1213, twen-

A group of Knights Templars leaves a castle for the Holy Land. French fresco from the twelfth century

ty years after the interdict, and the pope recognized the legitimacy of his children with Agnes, giving them rights to the throne.

Magna Carta

Philip Augustus's opponent, King John Lackland of England, tangled with the imperious Innocent III in an equally disagreeable way. In 1207, the pope had sent his enemy Stephen Langton as his legate and the archbishop of Canterbury. John resisted the appointment for years, but Innocent bided his time. When John needed the pope's assistance in 1212, facing trouble in his disputes with English nobles, his own vassals, he was forced to finally accept the appointment. John even agreed to become a vassal of the pope, in effect officially recognizing the doctrine of *dominium mundi*. Once the oath of fealty had been sworn, Innocent III whole-

heartedly supported his new vassal.

As the archbishop of Canterbury, Stephen Langton turned out to be a moderate man of great use in reconciling the king with his numerous enemies. The English nobles were fed up with always having to pay for his disasters. The defeat at Bouvines marked the turning point in their attitude. John's vassals repudiated their vows of fealty when the king next tried to raise money to finance a war. John did not stand a chance against his rebellious vassals. He was given a list of demands to which he reluctantly added his seal. Basically, they stated that the king was not allowed to impose taxes without his vassals' consent. A council of twenty-five would monitor compliance with the agreements. The document was finalized in John's chancellery. The indispensable Stephen Langton, who supported the king with some misgiving, ensured that it also included articles on the rights of the Church, the cities, and the people. The document is known as the Magna Carta or the Great Charter.

Even as copies were being sent throughout the country, John regretted his capitulation. He appealed to his liege lord, Innocent III. The pope promptly rescinded the entire charter because, in his opinion, it ran counter to the law and the rights of kings. This might have provoked civil war but for John's death shortly thereafter, in 1216, the ascendancy of a child, Henry III, to the throne, and the subsequent appointment of a regent. The Magna Carta was reestablished, making the war unnecessary.

Dominium mundi?

When Innocent died in 1216, he was at the peak of his power. All his enemies had been exposed to his ideas about the *dominium*, but there was some question as to the extent of their support for the concept. Otto had paid little heed to his agreement with the pope. Philip Augustus and John Lackland did not exactly display a keen sense of reverence toward him.

In 1204, the aggressive pilgrimage called the Fourth Crusade, which Innocent very much wanted, had degenerated into the sacking of Constantinople, with the Crusaders devastating the city and carrying off many of its treasures. The pope excommunicated the perpetrators, but it is not clear how sincerely he opposed the expedition. Innocent III never stopped dreaming of liberating Jerusalem from the Muslims. Less than a year before his death, he had managed to extract a promise for a Crusade from his ward Frederick. The young emperor would fulfill that promise but in a very different way from anything Innocent imagined.

Page from a medieval manuscript describing the laws governing popes and emperors

Rulers in Europe

Monarchs in the Thirteenth Century

Innocent had greatly enhanced the power of the papacy. It was evident in his condemnation of the sack of Constantinople, however, that his fourth crusade had gotten out of control. He had received assurance of another crusade from his pupil Frederick, the young heir to the Norman throne and the Holy Roman Empire.

While the pope was working on having his ideas on *dominium mundi* (sovereignty over the world) recognized, Frederick grew up surrounded by court intrigue. He wandered through the multilingual metropolis of Palermo (Sicily), hung out at the harbor,

visited synagogues and mosques, and bombarded passersby with a multitude of questions. His daily contact with the town's diverse population gave him fluency in Arabic and Greek. But Frederick could be amiable one moment and rude the next. He constantly assessed everything and everybody, developing into an encyclopedic scholar. A skeptical reader, he was familiar with the teachings of Muhammad as well as those of Jesus and Moses. He indicated more than once that he had not discovered the truth in any one of them. He admired Islam and its culture all his life, enjoying a

The document that Frederick II sent to Pope Honorius II, in which he describes his support for the union of Sicily with the German Empire

positive relationship with his Muslim colleagues. They sent him scholars and eunuchs (who served as security guards for the homes and women of Islamic rulers), valuable manuscripts and rugs, and most of the animals that made up his famous menagerie. He wrote a guide to falconry that could still be of use today.

A mystery to his subjects, Frederick became known as *stupor mundi* (the wonder of the world). He set out to continue the policies of his father and his grandfather, both of whom had died prematurely. His focus was on Italy. He had an aversion to what he saw as the uncivilized, cold north. He also had enough insight to realize that the power of the Hohenstaufen family had been undermined north of the Alps.

Frederick made a series of concessions confirming the status quo in Germany. He considered it prudent to let the Germans handle their own affairs, signing an agreement with the dominant nobles to that effect. In exchange for the freedom they were given, the nobles were willing to recognize his empire. The system worked very well. After the agreement with the nobles, Frederick made a final appearance in Germany when one of his sons rebelled.

Miniature from the *Chronicle,* written by the Italian Villani, depicting Frederick II capturing the city of Jerusalem

Left in Germany as his father's representative, this son, Henry, elected king of Germany in 1220, surrendered as soon as Frederick arrived in the north in 1235. Frederick sentenced him to a long, hard prison term in Italy. As he was being taken to a prison in Italy, Henry took the opportunity to jump into a ravine and kill himself. As usual, Frederick displayed neither sorrow nor regret.

In Italy, Frederick demanded complete authority over the entire peninsula. He established an absolute monarchy in the Norman kingdom. Every form of opposition was squelched through torture and bloodletting. The king demonstrated a sadistic preference for the putting out of eyes, castration, and burning. Frederick made the Sicilian Empire into the most modern state in the West. A well-oiled official machine governed the empire according to imperial

wish. He raised taxes, with the rich paying more than the poor. Although his direct levy was equitable, Frederick's subjects paid the highest taxes in the known world. That his people were also the most prosperous and the best protected against bandits made little impression on them. The "wonder of the world" was widely considered a tyrant.

In the early years of his reign, Frederick's relationship with Pope Honorius III was cordial. He even restored papal authority in central Italy, where local leaders had regained power since the death of Innocent III. Despite his promise to Innocent III, Frederick found no time for a crusade.

In 1227 however, Gregory IX, an extremely vigorous octogenarian, took over the seat of Saint Peter, reigning until 1241. His policies resembled those of Innocent III, a fact immediately brought home to Frederick. Gregory gave him the choice of

On the left, Pope Innocent IV at the Council of Lyons in France, during which it was decided that Frederick II would be excommunicated. Miniature from the thirteenth century.

excommunication or crusade. Frederick equipped and sent off a fleet, but an epidemic broke out in the crew. The fleet was forced to return home without success. Gregory did not believe Frederick's excuse and excommunicated him, his most powerful potential rival in Italy.

The next year, Frederick set out to sea again, despite the excommunication. The crusade had now become a matter of honor. In Palestine, he heard that he had again been excommunicated by Gregory, but once again, Frederick paid no heed. He had by then remarried. His new wife, Isabella, was the heir to the kingdom of Jerusalem. Frederick initiated negotiations with the sultan of Egypt. Frederick got Jerusalem back, in exchange for certain guarantees for the people of Islam. In 1229, the emperor was able to travel undisturbed to the Holy City to have himself crowned king.

After the coronation ceremony, Frederick returned to Sicily with little delay, installed his queen in the palace, and thereafter paid no attention to her. He had by now decided to assert his claims on the rest of Italy. Pope Gregory had resurrected the Lombard alliance, since both papacy and the independent cities had reason to fight Frederick's domination.

The war continued for the remaining twenty years that Frederick would still rule. In general, luck was with him. Innocent IV, who succeeded Gregory in 1243, even had to flee to France. In 1245, he tried unsuccessfully to organize a crusade against the excommunicated emperor.

Frederick was slowly gaining territory in a cruel war when, in 1250, just at the point he seemed to have the upper hand, he died.

Frederick II and his wife, Isabella, the daughter of the English king John Lackland

Pope Clement IV handing Charles of Anjou the fief of Normandy. Miniature from the thirteenth century.

1348

The Misfortune of the Hohenstaufens

Frederick's successor, Conrad IV, had been installed in Germany as his father's deputy in 1235. He crossed the Alps immediately to take over the estate. By then, not much was left of Frederick's good position. Over the remaining years of his life, Conrad did little to improve the situation. When he died in 1254, his son Conradin, who had remained in Germany, was still a child. Conrad's half-brother Manfred took over the leadership in Italy on his behalf, while the hereditary prince stayed in Germany.

Due to the deaths in the ruling family, all of northern Italy had gradually fallen back into the hands of the pope again. Only the Norman Empire in the south remained for Manfred to rule. It was not until 1258 that he was able to pick up where Frederick had left off, becoming a threat to the pope and the cities in Lombardy. By then, the entire House of Hohenstaufen had been excommunicated.

In 1263, the pope took it one step further: He granted the crown of the Norman Empire to Charles of Anjou, the brother of the French king Saint Louis IV. In 1266 Charles fought Manfred at Benevento. Manfred was killed, and Charles became the king of Sicily. Charles needed no great effort to consolidate power in the entire empire. The Ghibellines rebelled once more, but Charles beat back the resistance, in the process capturing the Ghibelline champion, the young Conradin. The prince was beheaded at the Palermo market while a great crowd looked on. The last member of the Hohenstaufens had come to an inglorious end.

Miniature from the thirteenth century depicting Charles of Anjou and Conradin dueling on horseback

English soldiers
from the thirteenth century,
on a miniature from the
Canterbury Psalter

Charles of Anjou

The Sicilian Empire by this time was now swarming with French immigrants. Charles decided to create a larger empire, which was to include the entire Mediterranean. To this end, with the aid of the recent arrivals from France, he extorted money ruthlessly from his subjects, rapidly becoming universally hated. The Sicilians paid, but Charles never really overcame the pope's subtle opposition.

Charles's subjects were assured that another dramatic conflict with the north would not be required. As Sicilians were celebrating Easter Monday in 1282, just outside Palermo's city gate where an exuberant crowd had gathered, a husband charged that an intoxicated Frenchman expressed a bit too much interest in his young Sicilian wife. The husband, offended and probably not too sober himself, attacked the Frenchman. A fight broke out between the two and the Frenchman collapsed, stabbed with a dagger. His fellow countrymen rushed to the scene from all directions to rescue him. Mass confusion and fervent anti-French feeling ensued, resulting in the mass murder known as the Sicilian Vespers. By that evening not a single Frenchman was alive within the city walls of Palermo. The tyrannical Charles was forced to retreat to Naples, on the southern part of the mainland.

Subsequently, the Sicilian notables were able to bring the revolution under control. They restored order and offered the crown of Sicily to King Peter of Aragon, who was married to a daughter of Manfred. After several years of useless posturing, Charles accepted the situation. He contented himself with control over southern Italy, while the kings of Aragon continued their rule over Sicily.

Everyone in Italy, except of course the ousted king, had reason to be happy. The

Louis IX (the Saint) kneels in prayer before relics of Christ. French miniature from the thirteenth century.

Norman Empire had been divided and could no longer seriously threaten the Lombard cities or the pope. Nobody was able to win the thirteenth version of the conflict between pope and emperor. The Holy Roman Empire went to rack and ruin as much as the papacy did, just the way Innocent had envisioned it. For years, the pope had taken part in a cruel war. His prestige had suffered as much from the war as it had from Frederick's attacks. In the end, it turned out that the papacy had lost a great deal of its earlier influence. Apparently, the *dominium mundi* was finally a thing of the past.

England: A Shift in Control

Under Henry II, England had seemed on its way to becoming the best-organized monarchy in western Europe, but the behavior of his sons, Richard the Lion-Hearted and John Lackland, as well as the subsequent government of Henry III (born in 1205 and reigned from 1216 to 1272) altered this trend. The continuous bickering over the feudal estates in France had already weakened the royal power. The English kings spent much time and money reconquering the areas under dispute, with one result being the increasing political power of the barons, the dominant nobility of the kingdom.

The barons, rather than attempting to undermine the monarchy, demanded a role for themselves, as representatives of the "community of the realm" within the royal government. This demand, reflected in the Magna Carta (in 1215), became more imperative later in the century. It put the barons in conflict with Henry III. He was forced around 1260 to forestall certain foreign policy issues in order to implement domestic restructuring in his government.

Henry's efforts to regain the power of the central monarchy were continued by his successor, Edward I, who reigned from 1272 to 1307. Changes in several areas occurred during the reign of Edward I. He targeted Wales, Ireland, and Scotland as likely areas for England's territorial expansion. They were closer to home, less costly to acquire, and able to be won without a fight with such powerful enemies as the king of France.

Edward's primary interest, however, was to put the barons back in their place. He tested the legitimacy of noble privileges in a number of lawsuits. Many of these privileges were based solely on oral tradition and had never been recorded in writing.

At the same time, he arranged for more meetings of "parliaments" during his reign. He invited not only the royal vassals, but also representatives of the lower nobility of the clergy and of the cities to these meetings. Clearly Edward considered the barons no longer the only representatives of the "community of the realm."

The barons' demands and the later activities of the parliaments indicate an important shift within the structure of government. In essence, this system was based on personal ties, particularly the direct relationship between the lord and his vassals. Each had their separate interests. The rapid evolution of the English monarchy contributed to the development of yet another interest, that of the populace as a whole. The barons were the first to indicate their support for the general interest. Edward then made it clear that other groups needed to become involved. This emphasis on social inclusion in the policy process marked the shift from a feudal to a territorial state.

France: A Saint on the Throne

While the pope and the Holy Roman emperor exhausted each other, the development of royal power in France continued unabated. If there was any opposition to the central power at all, it normally amounted to very

Miniature from the *Chronicle* of Villani, depicting Louis IX (the Saint) aboard a ship during the Seventh Crusade, which was aimed at the destruction of Tunis

little. The monarchy continued to consolidate its base. This was the situation in France when Louis IX assumed the reins of government in 1234, after a period of regency by his mother, Blanche of Castile.

Even during his lifetime, Louis was considered a saint, and not without reason. He was the only king of his time to use the ideology of medieval monarchy as a guide: he wanted to ensure peace, maintain order, and provide justice. When Pope Innocent III tried to convince him to join a crusade against Frederick II in 1245, the pope was clearly misguided. Louis refused to do battle against fellow Christian kings.

Louis's subjects had plenty of reason to be content. Their king did not participate in the typical political misadventures of the

ing had become commonplace even within the church. Trials by ordeal had been officially condemned as superstition by a council of prelates. Louis resolutely put an end to the practice in his realm. This made the king, already well respected, even more popular.

Though he was not universally loved, Louis's subjects believed that the monarchy protected them from injustice and exploitation. This was particularly true of the communes Louis championed despite hostility from the aristocracy. The people felt it was in their own interests to defend the monarchy's central authority. Louis's approach became known outside his realm, as well. His sense of justice was hailed throughout Christendom. It became almost standard practice to put difficult matters before Louis for consideration. The French king enjoyed passing judgment and his sentence was always accepted.

Louis did not die in his own country. Committed to the ideals of the crusades, he organized two expeditions, both of which failed. The first one, from 1248 to 1254, landed him in Egypt, where he spent five years but achieved little because of poor strategic judgment. The second crusade, from 1270 to 1272, went to Tunis. The campaign was quickly stranded when an epidemic broke out among the crusaders in the desert heat and Louis himself fell ill and died in 1270.

King Owl

Piety was not a permanent feature of the French monarchy. Louis's successor, Philip III (reigned 1270–1285), waged an unsuccessful campaign against Peter of Aragon, purely in order to support his uncle Charles. His son, Philip IV, who succeeded him in 1285, had the same aloof nature and features as Frederick II, notable for his cold eyes. Because of his handsome appearance, his subjects called Philip "the Fair," but his nickname in southern France was perhaps more appropriate: King Owl. Said the bishop of Pamiers: "The king is like an owl, the most beautiful of birds but worth nothing. He is the most handsome of men but he stares fixedly in silence."

Philip the Fair strove rigorously throughout his reign (1285–1317) to strengthen royal authority. He displayed similar aggression in foreign policy, waging war against England and against his own fief, Flanders. Those expeditions were costly. The king had to stave off bankruptcy his entire life. He tampered with government coffers, levied new taxes, and invented a number of schemes to fill the empty treasury. He ruined

On the left of this early fourteenth century miniature, Pope Boniface VIII hears witnesses pleading for the canonization of Louis IX (the Saint)

past which tended to victimize the common man. He turned out to be a responsible *pater familias* (family man), genuinely interested in law and civil justice. He streamlined legislation, took strong action against corruption in the administration of justice, and dispatched officials to supervise the actual application of his guidelines.

One such guideline was the prohibition of trials by ordeal, a remnant of Carolingian law, a practice that had claimed the lives of many innocent people. Although the practice had been condemned by the Fourth Lateran Council in 1215, judges still tried to have God indicate the guilty party by all kinds of tests and ritual duels. The townspeople were especially opposed to these practices, for many innocent merchants had succumbed to the brilliant fighting prowess of knights. Such experiences gave rise to doubts about the nature of God's intervention. In the thirteenth century, this question-

die ꝺ anno quo supra.

his reputation in the process.

His first victims were the French Jews. In 1306, Philip confiscated all their money and possessions, including even notes of debt obligation (IOUs) to them. Quite soon, many subjects were in debt to the king. In 1307, Philip needed additional funds. This time, the prosperous Knights Templars

became the victim. Gossip already abounded about crime and witchcraft within the order. This was encouraged, in part, by Philip, so that the royal theologians could accuse the knights of heresy and Philip could have the group prosecuted. Under the stress of the torture chambers, most Knights Templars admitted to the charges against

Spanish miniature from the end of the twelfth century, depicting a scene described in medieval lawbooks: the testimony of witnesses concerning the validity of a testament

them. The king had achieved his goal. The Knights Templars was dissolved and its possessions transferred to Philip. Even the money that French citizens had deposited with the tormented order disappeared into the treasury and was never seen again. While the Templar affair was still being wrapped up, Philip targeted the next group: the Lombard bankers. They had been imprudent enough to lend money to the king. Like the Jews before them, the Lombard bankers lost goods, money, and notes of debt obligation to Philip.

King Philip *versus* the Papacy

The considerable revenue of the Catholic church had always been exempt from taxes. Philip decided to modify his taxation policies to end this exemption. The French king was not unique in this decision. His enemy, Edward of England, was already taxing the

Pope Boniface VIII
(1294–1303)

Suit of armor of Philip IV
the Fair of France (1285–1314).
He was the son of Philip III
the Bold and Isabella of
Aragon and married Jeanne of
Navarre.

clergy, making it clear that defaulters would be treated as outlaws.

At the time, Pope Boniface VIII reigned (1294–1303) in Rome. He was a tough man, deeply convinced of his own holiness and the concept of *dominium mundi*. The idea of taxing the clergy ran completely counter to his beliefs, leading to tremendous conflict. Boniface forbade both Philip and Edward to implement their clerical tax policies. He issued a papal bull (or edict) in which he declared the right to correct such impious kings.

Philip circulated a falsified version of this edict, one which presented Boniface as demanding direct political authority for himself over the king. The French people, believing the propaganda, then sided overwhelmingly with their king. The pope subsequently issued another bull demanding both spiritual and temporal power, and the right to depose a king. The beneficiary was Philip. At court, a meticulous lawyer named Guillaume de Nogaret put together an elaborate suit against Boniface. The pope was accused, among many other things, of the murder of his predecessor and of keeping a devil in the house. Philip then convoked a synod of bishops. On the basis of the suit, it met in 1302 and demanded that the pope justify himself before a general council of prelates.

Guillaume was dispatched to Italy with an army of soldiers to capture Pope Boniface. Once within the papal state he had the support of the nobleman Sciarza Colonna, an archenemy of the pope and a strong opponent of papal authority. On September 7, 1303, Guillaume and his force took the pope by surprise, capturing him in his palace in the town of Anagni. Guillaume now had to find a way to get the pope out of Italy alive, because Sciarza demanded his blood on the spot.

A few days later, however, the townspeople of Anagni came to the defense of their pope, attacking the kidnappers and chasing them out of the country. The rescued Boniface returned to Rome, where he died a month later at the age of 86, probably as a result of his struggles. His successor Clement V came to an agreement with Philip, in fact giving in to the king altogether. Clergy were taxed, at least in France, and Clement also allowed Philip to disband and execute the Knights Templars, confiscating all their money. Philip even managed to have a Frenchman elected as the next pope.

It was clear that *dominium mundi* no longer had any meaning. The papacy had relinquished its position to the secular world leaders.

Relief from the Cathedral of Reims, France, showing a knight receiving Holy Communion before leaving for battle

The Late Middle Ages

The Transformation of the Medieval World

At the end of the thirteenth century, the development of European society ground to a halt. Land reclamation stopped, trading activities ceased to expand, and population growth stagnated. The annual fairs in Champagne, long the measure of economic activity, dwindled. The medieval community had reached a saturation point. With the existing structures and resources, any further growth had become impossible.

This stagnation was reflected in the political situation. In 1291, the city of Acre, last possession of the Crusaders in the Near East, was lost. The Christian reconquest of Spain from the Muslims ended. (Not until 1492 would the last Muslim ruler be ousted from southern Spain.) In eastern Europe, the borders of the Latin Christian world were

In the fourteenth century the Black Death swept across Europe in the largest outbreak of the plague in history, causing the death of one-third of the European population. This Flemish miniature from 1349 illustrates the large number of funerals held at the time.

threatened by Mongol attacks.

During the fourteenth and fifteenth centuries (the late Middle Ages), social disarray was rampant in Europe. Black Death, an epidemic of bubonic plague, destroyed a third of the population of western Europe around 1350. The destructive confrontation between England and France called the Hundred Years' War continued. The earlier

In a thirteenth-century English book illustration, a boy embraces the girl he loves

trend to centralized power and improved government seemed to have been reversed. Throughout Europe, feuds broke out among the nobility, while the heightened contrast between the classes led to a series of uprisings by farmers and merchants. Even the Church could not escape the consequences of this chaos. The popes lost their prestige when they decided to change their residence from Rome to Avignon, where they stayed for several decades. The situation was aggravated by a schism that produced a situation where two–and, for a short time, even three–popes were ruling concurrently. Criticism of the practices, wealth, and worldly attitude of the clergy became increasingly bitter.

Many historians are inclined to refer to this situation as the crisis of the late medieval world. It is perhaps more accurate to use the more neutral term *transformation.* It is certainly true that people experienced enormous distress during this period. Many lost hope and resigned themselves to waiting for the end of the world.

However, there were indications of a different sort at the same time. New trade centers sprang up, new forms of industry developed. Small Portuguese ships sailed along the west coast of Africa, from cape to cape, and from one southern port to another, in the hope of reaching the Indies. This was the start of the transformation from the feudal system of the Middle Ages to the kind of

society that would occur in the *Ancien Régime,* the political and social system of France before the Revolution of 1789.

Transformation of the Economy

The decline in the European population started in approximately 1300. This made it necessary to scale down production in order to adjust it to the decreased consumption. At the same time, a number of other changes in economic structure took place.

In the agricultural sector, production was increasingly geared to market demand. In some areas, this led to monoculture. For example, a large part of agriculture in England was dominated by the strong demand for exports of wool. On the other hand, farming in the Baltic was primarily devoted to producing grain for a large part of northern Europe. This increasing specialization of agricultural production in different regions stimulated commerce, both national and international.

The cities, in turn, developed their own export specialties. Competition between traditional sites and new centers of production increased. The old centers had focused on expensive quality products. Labor costs in these cities had become relatively high. The new centers consisted mostly of small, up-

A medieval town in Italy strategically built on the top of a hill. Such towns were often fortified.

The popes resided in the *fortified* monastery complex of St. John Lateran in Rome, on the spot where the first Christian emperor, Constantine, established a basilica. In 1309 Pope Clement V was forced to leave Rome for Avignon.

and-coming cities that had acquired a large labor force from workers who had moved in from rural areas. This made it possible to keep labor expenses relatively low, despite the upward trend. These new centers focused on the production of items of lesser quality, with a shorter useful life and a lower price tag.

The decline in population caused changes in the organization of labor. The increased demand for laborers led to great social and geographic mobility. This caused groups of craftsmen to protect themselves by forming guilds. In most of the commercial centers, the guilds became increasingly concerned with protection and exclusivity.

Map of Avignon by Franz Hogenberg (1573), on which the papal palace is prominently visible

The transformation of society that accompanied these developments generated great social tensions. In many cities, the proletariat (the laboring class) increased. The municipal property belonged to a small group of wealthy people, who developed into entrepreneurs. They did not take part in the production process, but organized, financed, and controlled it. The many conflicts during this period were provoked not so much by the poorer members of the population, but rather by the group above them, the middle class, who were threatened by the polariza-tion of property. In the rural areas, tensions increased as well. On the one hand, the farmers position was strengthened by the increased demand for laborers and the opportunities offered by the market. On the other, farmers were held in check by the great landowners, who used their power to maintain their dominant position.

The nobility, which for centuries had been the most important group and the backbone of the feudal system, was in trouble. Land did not generate enough revenue to cover the cost of living. The military monopoly was

View of Avignon, with the famous bridge over the River Rhone, and in the background the Palais des Papes, where the pope resided during the so-called Babylonian exile (1309–1377)

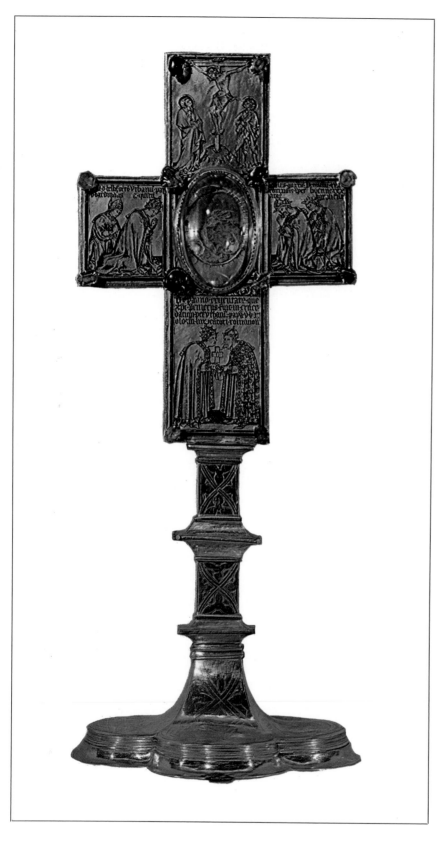

Reliquary cross
that Urban V (who was pope
from 1362 to 1370)
gave to the German emperor
Charles IV

under fire as well. The failure of the nobility became clearly apparent in the battle of Kortrijk (in present-day Belgium) in 1302, when an army of Flemish civilians wiped out an expensive, heavily armed battalion of knights. This was only a small taste of what was in store in the Hundred Years' War. It was a bloodbath in which many people perished. Heavily armed French knights were constantly being defeated by common English archers.

During this period, marked as it was by tensions and disasters, an increased desire for religion emerged. The dreaded epidemic of the Black Death, especially, led to great fear. Further horrors were anticipated, including the end of the world. Some people tried to avert disaster through asceticism, hoping to placate God. Others indulged themselves in every possible pleasure, "while it was still possible." If ever the Church was needed to channel these emotions, this was the time. Yet the Church itself was undergoing a transformation during this period—and the transformation was not a smooth one.

Statue of Boniface IX,
who was pope from 1389
to 1404,
in Rome

The Ecclesiastical Crisis: Corruption, Incompetence, and Schisms

The brave attempts of Hildebrand and his followers to reform the Church in the eleventh century were only partially successful and that success was temporary at best. Initially, the defeat of the emperor, Henry IV of Germany, seemed to anticipate a release from worldly influences in the Church, but the situation actually became much worse. The bishops' sees (cathedral towns), abbeys, and churches fell into the hands of local potentates who possessed sufficient information to blackmail–and therefore to control–the electoral boards. High ecclesiastical positions were usually very lucrative. Taxes, inheritances, and donations poured into the treasury.

Simony (the sale of church office) was rampant. Unworthy men gained profitable positions. All too often their hunt for lucrative sinecures (a position that requires little or no work and that usually provides an income) was successful. This resulted in a series of abuses. Bishops and abbots often exploited their positions, even selling the less prestigious appointments to the highest bidder. Sometimes they did not even bother to take up residence at their place of office and received the revenues at home.

During the thirteenth century, the papacy lost much of its authority. The last phase of the battle against the emperor greatly diminished the influence of the Holy See. Pope Boniface VIII (1294–1303), fenced in on all sides by rebellious noblemen, had been forced to yield the right to make clerical appointments to Philip the Fair. The election of his successor, Benedict XI, in 1303 was determined largely by the will of France.

Babylonian Captivity

Benedict XI died in 1304, shortly after his appointment. The cardinals then elected a Frenchman, who chose the name Clement V and prepared to leave for Rome. However, this preparation would last his entire rule. Rome was torn apart by quarrels between the noble houses. In Italy, a chaotic battle between the Guelphs and Ghibellines was in progress, which continued even after the house of Hohenstaufen was defeated. Clement V had little desire to become involved in this hornets' nest. He ended up in the city of Avignon, which, with the surrounding territory, had been given to the Holy See. In those years, Avignon was a part of the Holy Roman Empire, with the Rhone River forming most of the border that separated it from the area belonging to the French king. Clement was thus close enough to the French court to be able to rely on its protec-

tion, but far enough away to avoid becoming a tributary vassal.

For more than fifty years, the popes remained in Avignon. During this entire time, the papal throne was occupied by Frenchmen. Some historians claim that they

CLEMENS V P·M

were no more than instruments in the hand of the French court, but their politics were actually remarkably independent. The king was regularly forced to back down. This period was named the "Babylonian Captivity" by the brilliant poet Petrarch, who campaigned to have the popes return to the Vatican.

The popes moved their entire administration to the huge palace in Avignon. During

Portrait of Clement V, pope from 1305 to 1314

this "captivity," it took on enormous dimensions. The ecclesiastical bureaucracy had always been ahead of its secular counterparts. The intellectuals it employed wrote better and more beautifully than their colleagues at the courts. They had a special talent for procedures and, as would soon appear, for inimitable corruption. Avignon became a gigantic administrative office, where everyone knew his place and his duties. The working methods were bureaucratic and slow. Corruption worked its way up to the highest levels. Whoever looked to this administration for justice usually looked to the wrong place. The popes did not behave like shepherds of the faithful, but like politicians. Their principal occupation seemed to be the maintenance of this bureaucracy.

This required a certain shrewdness and perhaps some diplomacy but certainly no holiness. The bureaucracy swallowed up large amounts of money. The popes were constantly on the lookout for new sources of income that would let them stay afloat. They took possession of claims and inheritances, could easily be bribed, and practiced simony on a vast scale. This cost the Holy See much of its prestige. People were no longer prepared to accord the same respect to the papacy that their forefathers had. With increasing frequency, they stated openly that the

Church was ruled by unworthy people and reforms were necessary.

Rome was humiliated by the fact that the Holy Father did not want to live in the Holy City. With each new pope, and each new disappointment, the people became more rebellious. Prestige was not the only reason. After the popes left, the lucrative influx of pilgrims had dwindled. The return of the pope had become increasingly urgent.

An Italian Pope

By the time the Hundred Years' War began, Avignon was no longer a pleasant place to live. Although the city was outside the war zone, the wandering bands of soldiers that terrorized France had little respect for state limits. On one occasion, a company invaded the papal palace and refused to leave until an enormous ransom was paid.

At this same time, the anarchy around Rome was reduced by papal action. The popes were too intent on power to give up their authority in the Holy See. They dispatched energetic cardinals to bring order in the area. By the 1470s, papal authority in Italy had been sufficiently restored that the popes could again play a role in Italian politics. This greatly disturbed Rome's neighbors in the north. Under the leadership of the powerful city of Florence, an antipapal

Large cross that once belonged to Benedict XIII, pope from 1394 to 1417

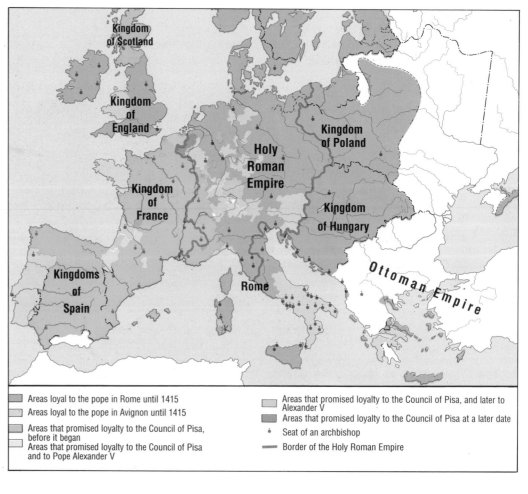

Areas loyal to the pope in Rome until 1415

Areas loyal to the pope in Avignon until 1415

Areas that promised loyalty to the Council of Pisa, before it began

Areas that promised loyalty to the Council of Pisa and to Pope Alexander V

Areas that promised loyalty to the Council of Pisa, and later to Alexander V

Areas that promised loyalty to the Council of Pisa at a later date

• Seat of an archbishop

— Border of the Holy Roman Empire

1364

league was formed. However, it encountered unexpected resistance.

In Italy, a movement arose demanding the pope's return to Rome. It was not the politicians who expressed this desire, but citizens and clergy who bombarded the pope, Gregory XI, in Avignon with petitions requesting his return. On one occasion, these petitions convinced him to move back to Rome, but his stay in the capital was such a

disaster that he soon fled back to Avignon. He finally returned to Rome to stay in 1377, dying there in 1378. The papal administration, as well as most of the cardinals, remained in Avignon. Only seventeen of them went to Rome.

The election of the new pope took place under threatening demands from the Roman people for an Italian pope. The fearful cardinals hastily chose the archbishop of Bari,

Painting by Domenico Beccafumi (1486–1551), depicting Saint Catherine of Siena receiving the stigmata, wounds similar to those inflicted on the crucified Jesus Christ

Miniature from the fourteenth century depicting Martin V being crowned pope during the Council of Constance

lid, influenced by popular intimidation.

A new election was held and the dissidents elected a different pope, Clement VII, who moved to Avignon. Urban, not surprisingly, did not accept this election. He remained in Rome and condemned the rebellious cardinals. This created a schism.

The competing popes issued contradictory decrees and hurled bulls of excommunication at each other. Christendom was in turmoil. The worldly rulers profited by the schism, recognizing the pope that best supported their interests. At first, Naples and France, and later Aragon, Castile, Portugal, Savoy, Scotland, and several German kings, took the side of Clement VII in Avignon. Northern Italy, England, Hungary, and the Scandinavian kingdoms took the side of Urban VI in Rome. Professors at the University of Paris advocated neutrality. This advice was followed by some kings and several religious orders.

In spite of the chaos, the schism had some positive effects. The existence of two popes made it clear that drastic reforms were needed. Intellectuals began to think about reform. Preachers became involved, unleashing tremendous religious enthusiasm. Some were accused of heresy when their preaching was combined with a cry for social revolution. In several places, reforms were instituted.

The schism lasted thirty-nine years, during which two powerful popes ruled in Avignon and five in Rome, each less fortunate than his predecessor. Urban used his talent for making enemies to excommunicate the king of Naples, who could have been a powerful ally. The same fate awaited Carl of Durazzo, who led a "crusade" within Italy to increase Urban's power. Finally, the pope was abandoned by the last of his cardinals. He died in 1389 unlamented.

The popes in Avignon did not fare well, either. After the death of Clement VII in 1394, the fanatical Pedro de Luna of Aragon came to power as Benedict XIII. He was a fierce ruler who spared no one, least of all the king of France. In 1398, this led to a siege by royal troops that forced him to flee to Perpignan and, later, to his castle in Aragon.

Christians sought a solution. The University of Paris stated the only one possible: One of the two popes would have to give up his position. Prominent Christians promoted negotiations between the two popes. Preliminary meetings took place at Marseilles, but the popes would not confront each other. The next solution was to let the two popes choose an independent tribunal. Both popes again refused to cooperate, and

who mounted the throne in 1378 as Urban VI. The cardinals in Avignon soon pledged their obedience. Once more, an Italian pope resided in the Holy City.

Schism

However, Urban, no diplomat, rapidly managed to make enemies of several of his own supporters. The newly hostile cardinals withdrew to Anagni in 1389, where they announced that the election had been inva-

Christians began to doubt their good faith.

Councils

A majority of the cardinals decided to hold a council in Pisa. This assembly of prelates found that the popes in Avignon and Rome were displaying signs of heretical stubbornness. It deposed them both and elected a new pope in their place. However, since neither of the other two popes was willing to step down, the church now had three popes. A dangerous precedent had now been established. For the first time, prelates had autonomously solved a problem without consulting the pope. This gave rise to the council theory, where a council was regarded as the highest ecclesiastical authority, even above the pope.

All three popes were fiercely opposed to this concept, even John XXII, the pope elected at Pisa. As the council theory gained popularity, John looked to the German emperor

The chapel in
the castle of Pope
Benedict XIII
in Peñiscola (Spain)

Louis of Bavaria for support. However, the emperor concluded that none of the three popes was worthy. He wanted a new council. A majority of the cardinals was in favor of the idea and so, under his auspices, a meeting was held in the city of Constance.

It was open to bishops and cardinals, university professors, and royal representatives. All were given the right to vote. In Constance, the council theory was explicitly formulated and accepted. John XXII, realizing that things were going against him, had no choice but to give up his position. Gregory XII, the pope of Rome, gave up his position voluntarily. It was impossible to

Fresco painted by Lorenzo Bicci in the Santa Maria Novella Church in Florence, depicting Pope Martin V surrounded by his flock

convince Benedict XIII to do the same, so the Council of Constance dismissed him. The pope and four loyal cardinals retreated to his castle in Aragon, where he spent the remainder of his life issuing bulls of excommunication against anyone who did not recognize him.

For the next two years, the Council of Constance was the ranking ecclesiastical authority. In 1417, the council chose a new pope: the wise cardinal Odo Colonna, who became Pope Martin V. He moved to Rome, far away from the council, and immediately distanced himself from the tenets of the council theory. Although he accepted certain reforms made by the council, he firmly rejected the idea that he had to submit to the decisions of the prelates.

The council, in response, issued a dangerous decree. Named after its first word *Frequency,* it provided that the council

would convene regularly. Martin did all that he could to sabotage Frequency, using papal envoys. The Council of Pavia, held several years after Constance, achieved nothing. However, Martin could not prevent the organization of a new assembly in the city of Basel. He died in 1431 before he was able to sabotage this council of Basel effectively. His successor, Eugenius IV, succeeded in doing so. When the Council of Basel demanded that he justify his actions, the pope simply moved the council to the Italian city of Ferrara. The moderates followed him. Only a small group of radical followers of the council theory was left behind in the Swiss city.

In Ferrara, Pope Eugenius IV scored a different type of diplomatic success. The Byzantine emperor Basil came to the West to enlist support against the powerful Turks and to discuss an end to the Schism of 1054. During the Council of Ferrara, the Eastern Church made so many concessions that unification was celebrated with elaborate ceremonies. Everyone was excited about the new unity–but nobody sent military support. In the final analysis, Byzantine discontent with unification caused its downfall.

The Council of Basel became more extreme. Finally, the remaining prelates could come up with only one solution: to dismiss the elected pope and elect their own pope. This decision gave the pope an excellent argument against council theory. He claimed that the churchmen in Basel had caused a new schism. Their claims simply led to further divisiveness within the ecclesiastic community. The pope insisted on the concept of his own supreme authority. A convinced Christianity accepted this and the council theory became obsolete.

Church unity was restored but the situation otherwise was virtually unchanged. Reforms were not implemented and only incidental improvements occurred. It was in the best interest of the popes to stop church reforms. During the remainder of the fifteenth century, they campaigned for public support in the manner of Italian kings seeking power in the area south of the Alps. They helped their followers obtain lucrative positions, appointed family members to high positions, led a life of luxury, and continued their old political conflicts.

As a result, the papacy fell further from its ideals, its ecclesiastical leadership jeopardized as its secular rule under *dominium mundi* had been. Clergy and laymen alike began to doubt if the papacy could really be reformed.

Jewish Culture in the Middle Ages

Keeping Their Own Identity

Miniature from a
fifteenth-century Belgian
manuscript on the subject of
the Passover seder,
the sacred meal during
which Jews celebrate the flight
of their people from Egypt

As a religious people, the Jews had an exceptional position in medieval society. Although the Christianity that dominated western Europe had its origins in the monotheism of Judaism, Jews constituted an isolated religious minority, existing largely outside the prevailing social system. They denied, of course, the fundamental tenet of Christianity, that Jesus Christ was the Messiah. Not allowed to function in the Christian-permeated system of government of Europe, they played a dominant role in finance and commerce, especially in the thirteenth century. This led to an ambivalent image of the Jews, who were thought of as either valued suppliers of essential materials or usurers.

In the eleventh century, the negative aspect of this ambivalence clearly predominated. The emphasis put on purity, unity, and homogeneity within the Latin Christian world by the reform movement of this time drew unfavorable attention to non-Christian minorities. The Jews were the first victims. The Crusades and the fanaticism they unleashed provoked extensive persecution of the Jews in the Rhineland in 1096, even though local bishops protested emphatically against it.

From that period on, the Jews' isolation was reinforced. They were often prevented from joining such social organizations as the guilds and from holding administrative offices. They were housed in separate quarters and were not allowed to have Christian employees. The Fourth Lateran Council in 1215 decreed that they must be identified as Jews by wearing the star of David on their clothing. They lost their advantage in finance and commerce to others, notably the Lombards. In subsequent centuries, they were banned from a steadily increasing number of countries: England, France, Provence, and Spain. The isolation of the Jews often caused serious misconceptions about them, similar to the contemporary ideas about heretics and, later, about witches. They were alleged to have entered a pact with the devil to destroy Christianity and were regularly accused of desecrating such ecclesiastical objects as relics of the saints and the host, the wafer used in the Christian rite of communion. During periods of insecurity, these accusations often produced new, more extensive persecutions. The most notorious out-

A miniature from the Middle Ages showing Jacob on his way to Egypt

Greeks under the Roman Empire, they were completely self-sufficient from an administrative and cultural standpoint. From their native land, they brought an intact culture and a legal system which had reached full maturity over the preceding centuries.

Their civilization and their legal system were bound by their common source, religion. The scripture of Judaism is the Hebrew Bible, which Christians call the Old Testament. The first five books, known as the Pentateuch, are particularly sacred. The religion and Jewish social customs rest, as well, on the Talmud, a voluminous work containing the essence of an oral tradition transmitted from generation to generation and written down around AD 200 to 400. The Talmud (which means "teaching" in Hebrew) contains the essence of Judaic law as well as historical, scientific, and medical information, proverbs, folklore, religious and moral sermons, and essays on biblical interpretation.

Because every detail of the Jewish legal system was based on biblical laws, it was of a predominantly religious character. Studying this material was the first task–and a practical necessity–for every Jew. After the diaspora, the Jewish community was based on this system, which had arrived in northern France and the Rhine region by way of Italy. It settled all practical and theoretical problems among Jews and the non-Jewish world.

Study of the Talmud was not the monopoly of a small elite, although it did constitute a career for a rather large group of the population. Education was characteristic of Jewish life. At the end of the tenth century, two eminent Jewish scholars reported that in most Jewish communities the number of educated Jews greatly exceeded that of the non-Jewish lower class. The total number of northern European Jews was small, but most of the men spent at least part of their time on religious studies.

This broad dissemination of learning is one reason why these early communities, which were within the cities of northern Europe, but in separate neighborhoods, had no rabbis. No one was considered a spiritual

rage took place around 1350 in connection with the Black Death, for which the Jews were thought responsible, and during which they were accused of poisoning water supplies.

An Emphasis on Learning
Despite their difficult situation, the Jews in medieval Europe applied themselves with great zeal to their culture. After the fall of the temple of Jerusalem in AD 70, the Jews had founded settlements in the religious and cultural dispersion called the diaspora. Like the

1370   Two wooden pointers, or *yads* (Hebrew word meaning "hand"), used to unroll and carry the Torah

leader, and there was no absolute authority on religious matters. Talmudic Jewry did not have a separate clergy. On the contrary, every Jew was the same from a religious point of view. Not until the fourteenth century was the rabbinate introduced as an office, for practical reasons. However, there were a number of excellent teachers who were appreciated by their students. An important example was the head of the Yeshiva, a Jewish academy.

Both religious and secular power were in the hands of the community, or *kehillah*, which acted as legislator, judge, and administrator. In internal and certain external matters, the Jews had almost complete autonomy. Every detail of their political, economic, social, and cultural life was determined by their own Talmudic laws. Judaic learning was a prerequisite for life.

The Bible and the Talmud

The most important school arose from the inspiration of a man whose comments are still valuable today, Rabbi Shlomo Yitzaki, known as Rashi. He was probably born at Troyes in France around 1040. For a number of years, he studied at the Yeshivas in Worms and Mainz. After some time, he was forced to take over the family business, managing the vineyard in Troyes.

In his commentary on the Bible, Rashi combined four areas which had been studied separately until that time: the correct spelling, pronunciation, and intonation of Hebrew; the meaning of certain passages, on

the assumption that the student is familiar with the grammar, syntax, and etymology (the derivation of words); biblical interpretation for advanced students who have read all the previous commentaries; and anagogic, or the highest level of spiritual interpretation,

In Europe Jews played important roles as merchants and money changers since observers of other religions were forbidden to deal in money in such a way. Seen as outsiders by anti-Semites, they were often persecuted and falsely accused, especially in times of crisis. This Spanish miniature shows a Jew being released after having been wrongly arrested.

Interior view of the synagogue in Prague (Czech Republic), the oldest synagogue in Europe

Title page of a thirteenth-century Jewish manuscript of the Book of Numbers, the fourth book of the Pentateuch

The fact that Rashi spoke Hebrew when he taught his students caused some difficulty. It had ceased to exist as a spoken language. Jews spoke the language of the country they lived in and regarded it as their own. Rashi provided a French translation for rare and technical words that is of tremendous importance. It represents the earliest documentation of Old French and includes hundreds of French words unknown elsewhere.

This great tradition of scholarship was to be cruelly interrupted by the Crusades and the misery they created. Only in present-day Israel has it been possible for the Jewish community to be reunited with the sacred traditions that medieval Jews were obliged to abandon.

History and Poetry

Because of the uncertain situation of the Jewish community, the result of recurring persecution, religious rites and traditions were recorded. Memory books, listing the names of Jewish martyrs, were begun. They are an important source of knowledge about Jewish history. In the twelfth century, for example, Efraim bar Jakob of Bonn, persecuted as a boy, describes the horror of the Crusades in an extensive report. He also expresses his misery in poetry. Poetry was used not merely to express the grief of the survivors, but to celebrate the Jewish high holy days.

Mysticism

Jewish mysticism (a striving for direct, intense communion with the divine) is esoteric, that is it includes secret doctrine meant for initiates. For this reason, the Jewish mystics of the twelfth and thirteenth centuries were called Cabalists. Here, the word *Cabala*, which basically means the handing down of tradition, must be understood to mean the transmission of secret knowledge. Medieval Cabalists sought to resolve such questions as the connection between God and creations and the nature of and reason for good and evil; they sought a path to spiritual perfection.

Jewish mysticism was not a marginal phenomenon; on the contrary, it developed at the center of the rabbinical Judaism that emerged at the beginning of the Christian era. Medieval Jewish mysticism, too, experienced its greatest flowering in the major centers of Jewish life and scholarship: the Rhineland and Provence.

Mysticism was also practiced by the sect known as the Hasidim. In the Rhineland, the Kalonymus family was the principal exponent of Hasidism. *Hasid* is the Hebrew word for "pious" (not to be confused with the

used primarily in sermons. Rashi wrote a commentary on the Talmud. His great work presents a wealth of information written in a succinct style that makes even the most difficult reasoning comprehensible.

The study of the Bible was based on the Palestinian tradition with its partly literal, partly anagogic explanation. The yeshivas, where these studies were undertaken, were mainly connected with the synagogues at Mainz, Worms, and Cologne in the Rhineland and Paris, Arles, and Narbonne in France. Jewish knowledge was not confined to one specific group. The yeshiva was a gathering place, an academic center, where young and old met to study the Bible and the Talmud.

modern sect, founded in the eighteenth century). According to legend, the very influential Kalonymus family had come to the Rhineland from Italy at the invitation of the Carolingians. They introduced Germany not only to the Talmud, but also to mysticism, which had already made its way to Italy from the Near East a long time before.

The first historical appearance of the Cabala, in Provence, also took place among the leading families of that region, who possessed the highest possible level of education, erudition, and piety. To some extent they could be referred to as "radicals" from a religious point of view. In fact, the pre-Christian Hebrew had used the word *Hasid* to apply to Jewish radicals.

Inspiration

These two movements, Hasidism in the Rhineland and Cabalism in Provence, are closely related to the historical situation of the age. German Hasidism originated in the era of the persecutions which erupted during the Crusades of 1096 and 1147 and in the subsequent period of torture and exploita-

Jewish cemetery in Prague. Because the Jewish religion does not allow grave sites to be disturbed, even tombs dating from medieval times remain untouched.

Jewish marriage certificate from Venice (1524). In medieval times Jews lived in separate parts of the cities, called ghettos. Marriages between Jews and Christians were not allowed.

1373

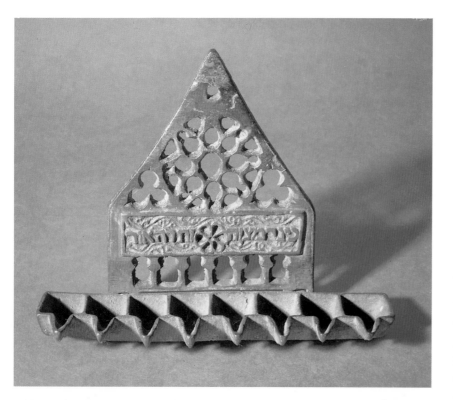

ditional Jewish practices, but they had a different view of the world and different expectations of the future.

The same applies to the appearance of the cabala in the twelfth century in Provence, which was the center of Catharism, the most important and most far-reaching heresy known to medieval Christianity. It had reached its zenith during that time, shortly before the crusade against the Cathars and the foundation of the papal inquisition destroyed the movement.

Numerology

The new approach was expressed mainly in biblical exegesis. Traditional biblical interpretation was based on the discussions collected by the rabbinical schools at the beginning of the Christian era in Palestine and Babylonia. In the twelfth century, this method had been perfected by Moses ben Maimon, known as Maimonides, on rational philosophical principles.

The mystics added a new dimension to this literal, scientific exegesis. Relying heavily on numerology, they introduced a new connection between words and sentences, and between divine names and characteristics which otherwise would not have been possible. Jewish mysticism is therefore largely concerned with the Torah, the first five books of the Old Testament. In other words, it is a mystical explanation of the divine revelation on Mount Sinai.

But Jews not only tried to reach their god through mystical biblical exegesis and revelation. They also tried to communicate through mystical prayer. "In the Torah, God speaks to people; in prayer, people speak to God."

Etching by
Rembrandt van Rijn
(1606–1669) depicting
a scene in the Jewish synagogue in Amsterdam.
He frequently used the
Jews of Amsterdam as models
for Old Testament figures
in his work.

tion. The crusaders had decided to wrest the Holy Land from the hands of the infidel, but they decided that they should first rid themselves of the enemy in their own home–the Jew who refused to recognize Christ as God. The ensuing fanaticism resulted in the disruption of Jewish society and deeply shocked the inner religious world of the Jews.

This trend was certainly connected with the numerous heretical Christian movements that the Jews encountered on their way to France, Italy, and Germany. Their ideas were not necessarily derived from these movements, but there was an analogous rejection of established tradition. These Jews certainly were not heretics; they did not reject tra-

The Hundred Years' War is the (inaccurate) term that is used to describe the wars between England and France waged from 1337 to 1453. This miniature depicts English soldiers defeating a French convoy carrying supplies for the beleaguered city of Orléans.

The Hundred Years' War

A Century of Blood and Misery

France and England had a long history of conflict, eight centuries of hostilities that would continue until the early twentieth century. The most terrible phase of their battle was the long series of campaigns and truces, misnamed the Hundred Years' War, that consumed France during the fourteenth and fifteenth centuries.

The Hundred Years' War was essentially the last stage of the battle that had begun in the twelfth century. The Peace of Paris in 1320 ended the conflict between France and Flanders; the Peace of Arras in 1435 officially ended the Hundred Years' War, but the English renewed hostilities in the 1440s, which continued until 1453, though there was much peaceful interaction.

The Hundred Years' War primarily affected noncombatants. Its warriors murdered and plundered, depopulated entire regions, razed towns, and destroyed the economic foundation of society. Charles VII chased the last Englishman into the sea, only to reign as king of a poorhouse.

Following the death of Charles VII, French lawyers determined that scions of the Valois branch were the closest relatives to the old dynasty, and the crown was given to Philip VI of Valois. Edward III claimed the crown as the son of a sister of the late French king, while Philip was only a cousin. The French cited Salic Law, that precluded a woman inheriting the throne or passing the inheritance on.

The succession issue, however, was only one source of controversy. English kings still owned fiefs in France, despite their annexation by the French under Philip Augustus.

Furthermore, the English had major economic interests on the French continent. Guienne, the region around Bordeaux, guaranteed a steady supply of cheap wine. The textile weavers of Flanders were dependent on English wool, an economic tie that was in sharp contrast to the political realities. The count of Flanders, Louis de Nevers, was an obedient vassal of the French king. In the event of a conflict with the king, the count might prohibit the importation of English wool and seriously damage the English economy. On the other hand, the English king

Edward III of England meets Philip VI of France.
Miniature from the *Chroniques de France*

1376

might impoverish Flanders by issuing a ban on wool exports.

The rich and powerful Flemish burghers were sympathetic to the aspirations of the English court and its supply of raw materials. Furthermore, England was an important market for Flemish textiles. The English king encouraged the burghers' rebellions against the Francophile count.

The hostilities began in 1337 when French King Philip VI again declared King Edward dispossessed of his French fiefs. Edward immediately proclaimed himself the king of France. The Flemish count ordered the arrest of all Englishmen residing in his realm. Edward replied by bringing wool exports to an immediate halt, resulting in massive unemployment in the Flemish towns. In Ghent, the workers rebelled. The uprising caught on in other cities and the count was forced to flee to France in 1339.

The Ghent aristocrat and merchant Jacob van Artevelde had become the leader of the rebels and took control of Flanders after the count was defeated. His ideal was a close federation of city republics under the protec-

tion of an English king officially recognized as the ruler of France. In February 1340, Edward III landed on the Flemish coast. In June, an English squadron swept a French fleet from the estuary of Sluys near Bruges. This ensured the undisturbed export of wool.

Jacob van Artevelde did not realize his ideal. French agents actively promoted dissension among the Flemish. The urban aristocracy turned against the guildsmen who constituted the backbone of the rebellion. The count returned to Flanders with the support of the lower rural nobility. The tyrannical Jacob van Artevelde had increasing difficulty maintaining his position. During a weavers' rebellion in 1345 in Ghent, van Artevelde was murdered by the crowd, freeing the count to restore his power. King Edward now focused his attention on regions to the south.

Crécy

Although Guienne in Bordeaux was an English foothold, it was occupied by the French, so Edward could not have used it as a foothold. Edward chose a shorter route in

Picture from a medieval manuscript showing the French king John the Good taken prisoner after the Battle of Poitiers (1356). He was sent to England and locked up in the Tower of London.

1377

The text of the testament of Charles V of France, with his personal seal attached

attacking France in July 1346. He landed at the Cotentin, Normandy, plundered Caen, and advanced rapidly to the region around Paris. Finding it impossible to conquer the French capital, he was forced to turn north. He positioned his troops for battle on the road to Dunkirk near Crécy. Near Crécy, the French cavalry charged the English ranks on August 26, 1346. It was the first time the French had been confronted by such military might. Edward had brought an army of 10,000 men armed with the new longbow, trained in the military tradition of centuries of battles against the Scottish and the Welsh.

Crécy was a disastrous defeat for France that enabled Edward to conquer the strategically located port of Calais. Edward was willing to settle for a truce to end the costly war. The victory at Crécy coincided with the defeat of his followers in Flanders.

The result was a new English foothold on the continent. When the war resumed, Edward's son, also named Edward, called the Black Prince for the color of his armor, destroyed vast regions of France in 1355. He directed his attacks south of Bordeaux up to Languedoc, then turned north and destroyed the French troops massed at the Battle of Poitiers, on September 19, 1356. King John II (the Good), successor to Philip V in 1350, was taken to a luxurious London prison.

Poitiers marked a second major blow to traditional knightly combat. In an attempt to imitate English tactics at Crécy, the French knights dismounted and waded through muddy terrain before being massacred by English soldiers.

Picture showing the Battle of Poitiers (1356). Though outnumbered by the French, the English won this battle.

1378

Chaos, Rebellion, Misery

The capture of John the Good heralded the beginning of four years of riots in France. Tension began during a session of the States-General meeting in 1357, called to find a solution for France's dire financial straits. The Paris provost of merchants, Etienne Marcel, wanted to grant political authority to the meeting. His rhetoric was successful. The states founded a commission to determine who was responsible for the defeats. The crown prince, who would later rule as Charles V, reluctantly signed a document announcing a major program of administrative reform.

After the States-General disbanded, the royal court again became the sole center of power. With a few followers, Etienne Marcel assumed the city's government. He ruled efficiently, organizing the citizens into military companies. The city had no plans of yielding just yet.

Charles gave orders to the nobility to fortify their castles against an English attack. In the country north and northeast of Paris, the peasants moved through the rural areas raiding their lords' castles, decimating noble families, and killing everyone they considered their opponent. Although the uprising alarmed the big landowners, the movement had little chance of success. The peasants had no real plan and were not well organized. Within a few weeks, the riot was over.

Charles II (Charles the Bad), king of Navarre, was responsible for restoring order. He had presented himself as regent. The landowners were grateful, but his archenemy, Etienne Marcel, considered it a dangerous development.

Outside of Paris, Charles V, who had left the city after the assassination of his marshals, could muster the support of honest monarchists who did not tolerate restrictions of royal power. They identified the crown with opposition to the English. When the crown prince advanced to Compiègne and called a session of the States of Champagne, seeking money, they gave it to him. Etienne Marcel began to lose his following. In 1358, he was killed by a monarchist.

Charles V then returned to a monarchist Paris, devoted to foreign policy. Edward III had slowly penetrated Burgundy. Charles realized that his weakened kingdom had little chance against mighty England. He started negotiations in 1360 that resulted in the Treaty of Bretigny. In exchange for a third of France, Edward relinquished his claims to the French throne. The political situation that existed during the reign of Henry II was now essentially restored.

The new ruler, although sickly, had shown his ability to resolve a crisis, was a clear thinker, and had admirable perseverance. Charles also was surrounded by able counselors who treated government almost as if it were a science.

The king entrusted his army to Bertrand du Guesclin of Gasconyo. The length and extent of the war had forced the fighting parties to recruit mercenaries from very different backgrounds who, after the Peace of Bretigny, became a luxury and were dismissed. They prowled the roads as highway

Miniature from the *Chroniques de France* depicting the coronation of Charles V of France and his wife, Johanna of Bourbon

Tomb effigy of Edward, the son of Edward III, named the Black Prince

robbers and ravaged all France. This kept up until Charles V chose sides in the civil war then raging in Castile, and Bertrand du Guesclin gathered the highway bands to lead them across the Pyrenees. In Castile they learned to battle on flat terrain and ran into their old enemy, the Black Prince.

Charles was working on rebuilding his country. The French people bestowed on their king the honorific of the "Wise." In 1367, Charles renewed the war. The Parliament of Paris, the highest court in France, declared the peace unlawful, thus making war again a fact of life. Actual hostilities started only three years later.

Military strategy had changed with Guesclin's highwaymen and their guerrilla tactics. They avoided the main troops of the Black Prince, who was exhausted from besieging strong fortifications while his highwaymen took possession of the country-

Richard II of England hands his regalia to the duke of Lancaster, who became King Henry IV. Miniature from the *Chroniques de France*.

side. The new battle tactics succeeded. In 1375 the English held the citadels of Bordeaux, Bayonne, and Calais. A year later, the Black Prince died and was succeeded by Edward III. The war seemed to shift to France's advantage.

In 1380 a new crisis forced both countries to suspend their war activities. Charles the Wise died, and England and France entered a maelstrom of rebellion and civil war.

Discord

In Paris the twelve-year-old Charles VI ascended the throne. His opponent, King Richard II of England, was also a teenager, placing both countries in the power of cantankerous regents.

England was experiencing great social upheaval. The peasants, the craftsmen, and some of the lower clergy were ready to fight. Under the bold leadership of Wat Tyler, they made their way to London, where they took over the political situation until quashed by the well-to-do middle class and the aristocracy.

In France, bands of robbers ravaged the land. Repeated epidemics decimated the population. The French king, Charles VI, went progressively insane. He was functional only for short periods at a time. During Charles's minority, the king's three uncles, all dukes, had served as guardians and advisors. The severity of Charles's madness only became apparent in 1393, by which time his younger brother Louis, made duke of Orléans in 1392, was old enough to rule and was named regent in 1393.

In England a parliamentary revolution robbed King Richard of his authority in 1399. When the young ruler appeared to be reckless and power-hungry, Parliament passed the crown to his cousin Henry IV of Lancaster, who ruled as Henry IV.

In 1404 in France, Charles's uncle Philip the Bold, duke of Burgundy, died. This exacerbated the conflict because his son, the unscrupulous John the Fearless, not taking into account the popularity of his opponent Louis of Orléans, had him killed in 1407. Louis's followers grouped around his relative, Bernard of Armagnac, prepared to take revenge on the party of the Burgundian duke. This was the start of the bloody conflict between the Armagnacs and the Bourguignons. Paris experienced uprisings under the leadership of the butcher Caboche and his *cabochiens*, who counted on the protection of John the Fearless. The well-to-do citizenry chose the side of Armagnac. The duke of Burgundy obtained support from a military alliance with the English, beginning the last phase of the Hundred Years' War.

This was, in fact, a civil war in which the English chose sides.

La Grande Pitié du Royaume

Henry V of England was a fickle, sly, and cruel man, yet because of his heroic deeds, was popular with his subjects. In 1415 he landed on the Normandy coast, took Rouen,

and destroyed the Armagnac cavalry at Agincourt in the largest battle of the war. Though less decisive than Crécy or Poitiers, it has been studied more, since thousands of French were lost, compared to only five hundred English, who were outnumbered.

John the Fearless was able to restore his influence in Paris. He overpowered Charles VI. The Armagnacs gathered around Crown Prince Charles VII while the French people were in great confusion. The alliance

This miniature shows King Charles VI of France on the left; he was married to Isabella of Portugal.

1382

between John the Fearless and the king of England had caused vehement indignation. In 1419 the Burgundian duke was killed by an Armagnac. John the Fearless and young Charles had agreed to meet on the bridge at Montereau, outside of Paris. But supporters of both began to hurl insults and draw swords, and the duke was slain.

The murderer had not served his side well. Philip II the Good, who succeeded his father as duke of Burgundy, was perhaps an even greater Anglophile. In fact, King Henry became lord and master of France. The frivolity of Queen Isabella, the wife of the mad king, raised doubts about the legitimacy of Crown Prince Charles VII. Isabella made matters worse by acknowledging Henry V as heir to the French throne in the treaty of Troyes. Things appeared to be finished for Crown Prince Charles in 1422, but the almost simultaneous deaths of Henry and Charles VI offered new opportunities.

Since the new king of England, Henry VI, was only nine months of age, the duke of Bedford was appointed regent. He controlled the French regions in his domain from Paris. Charles VII held court in the small town of Bourges, from where he conducted a rather ineffective government. His enemies deprecatingly called him the king of Bourges as his pessimism spread throughout France, with the people giving up hope after experiencing misery, oppression, and poverty. These were bleak times.

Yet there was a flicker of hope. Even if it was true that God had punished France for its sins, the pious felt, He would not permit the destruction of the country of Charlemagne and Saint Louis. Only against this backdrop can the victory of Joan of Arc, the Maid of Orléans, be explained, coming as it did at the last possible moment. Led by the duke of Bedford, English troops set upon the conquest of the city of Orléans following another great victory at Verneuil. The occupation would enable them to connect the Anglophile regions north and south of the Loire River. In 1427, the duke of Salisbury besieged the city. For two years the French captain warded off the attacks of the English army. The lord of the city, Charles of

Richard II and his company in a boat. Richard was the son of Edward the Black Prince. His first wife was Ann of Bohemia. After she died he became engaged to the seven-year-old daughter of the French king Charles VI. Miniature from the *Chroniques de France.*

The assassination of Louis of Orléans by supporters of John the Fearless in 1407. This act led to a period of fierce civil war in France. Miniature of Enguerrand de Monstrelet in a manuscript from the fifteenth century, called the *Chronicle.*

Joan of Arc, the peasant girl who led the French army, on her way to Reims. She was later condemned as a heretic and burned at the stake.

Orléans, had been captured by the English at Agincourt and, according to the standards of chivalry, it was considered treason to attack the regions of an imprisoned lord. Orléans was seen to be bravely fighting "criminals," and the city's resistance grew to become the symbol of France's struggle. In the spring of 1429, when the starving city seemed close to surrender, the Maid appeared.

Joan of Arc (born 1412), the daughter of a peasant family with many children, had never gone to school. At the age of thirteen she started to have visions and heard what she called voices—the voices of Saint Michael, Saint Catharine, and Saint Margaret, directing her to go to France in the name of God. The Barrois was located in Lorraine, at that time a fiefdom of the Holy Roman Empire and not considered a part of France. The voices ordered her to relieve Orléans and to have Charles VII crowned king in Reims.

Firmly convinced that she was carrying out God's will, Joan of Arc won her family's

compliance and contacted a nearby military authority who sent her to the duke of Lorraine. The duke recommended her to the French king. Joan of Arc traveled with six relatives to Chinon, where Charles VII was staying. He had already received a letter explaining the purpose of her coming.

An ecclesiastical commission was created in Poitiers to investigate the case of Joan of Arc. Following a favorable report, the king was able to raise an army with his last funds. Joan was able to inspire the soldiers with

great enthusiasm. They breached the blockade of Orléans. Ten days later the English ended the siege of the city. Charles VII sent a letter to all cities, announcing the miracle.

Joan's task had not yet been completed, however. Charles remained to be crowned in Reims, then in the possession of the Burgundians. Led by the duke of Alençon and Marshal de la Hire, the French armies easily cleared the way. De la Hire destroyed an entire English force near Patay. On July 17, 1429, Charles was crowned in the Cathedral at Reims and Joan announced that her task had ended.

At the insistence of her comrades in arms, however, she decided to remain in the king's service until Paris was liberated. The attack on Paris failed and the Maid suffered a thigh wound. Charles VII again refused to act. Joan urged in vain that the expedition be pur-

Henry V of England gained a great victory over the French at the Battle of Agincourt. The battle was also historic because a large army of foot soldiers from the lower classes defeated the knights of the French nobility.

The siege of the French city of Orléans. The English beleaguered the city for two years. When Joan of Arc succeeded in bringing in new troops, the English gave up and the city was liberated.

sued forcefully. Aided by a small detachment, she began to carry out small raids on the enemy. She was taken prisoner by the Burgundians in May, 1430, near Compiègne and fell into the hands of Cauchon, the bishop of Beauvais. She was extradited to the English. Joan was transferred to Rouen, where a lengthy trial for heresy took place, presided over by Cauchon. She was open to the charge of heresy by the mere fact of being a woman who wore armor to lead a military campaign, claiming visionary instruction from God. Controlled by the English and wanting to oppose the committee of learned men of Poitiers, the University of Paris spoke out against her. The Maid spent the last few months of her life threatened and tortured. Finally she was forced to sign a misleading statement branding her a heretic, apostate, and servant of pagan gods.

She was burned at the stake in Orléans, persisting in her innocence until the end. After her death Joan of Arc posed a greater threat than during her lifetime, for the English had created a martyr, as Joan of Arc became the symbol of French resistance against English domination.

Soon the duke of Burgundy, Philip the Good, contacted Charles, predicting a bad outcome for the English. This resulted in the Treaty of Arras (1435), which made the reconciliation a fact (as it had been one of Joan of Arc's ideals). It implied that Philip would withdraw from the war in exchange for Auxerre, Boulogne, and the fortresses along the Somme. Furthermore, Charles would officially condemn the murder of John the Fearless and would dismiss Philip from his obligations as a vassal for life.

Following Arras, the position of the English in France became more critical by the day. Six days prior to the treaty's conclusion, the duke of Bedford died. His two successors were unable to agree on anything, and King Henry VI turned out to be mentally deficient. Charles's commanders undertook incursions deep into English territory. In 1436 the city of Dieppe defected, and in the same year a French captain led his troops into Paris. The Parisians expelled the English garrison. Influenced by his lover, Charles VII started an implacable guerrilla war. This method of warfare exhausted the English troops as much as it did the French treasury.

Weariness with the war finally resulted in the Truce of Tours, which did not result in permanent peace. When the English mounted attacks on the Francophile duke of Brittany in the 1440s, because this had been English-controlled territory and they and the many loyalists among the populace wanted to retain it, Charles ended the truce.

The Last Phase

The goal of the new campaign was the conquest of Normandy. The people of Normandy had officially called in Charles's aid and the French king was happy to oblige. In October 1449 Rouen capitulated, followed by Cherbourg in August of 1450.

Only Guienne remained loyal to the English. The population was still solidly with the English, who had ruled there for centuries without interruption. Bayonne surrendered in 1451, but Bordeaux changed hands twice before falling into French hands two years later. England had been driven from the entire continent. Only Calais, surrounded by Burgundian territory, still had an English garrison. For the time being, a civil war in England rendered all attempts to reconquer France impossible.

The English conquering Rouen during the reign of Henry V

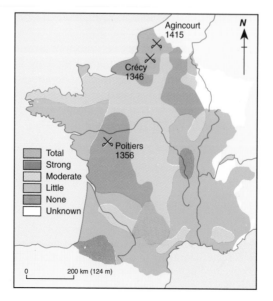

The destruction caused by the Hundred Years' War in France, 1337–1453

A banquet given by Charles VI of France in honor of Charles VI of Germany. On the right, a theatrical reenactment of the crusaders' siege of the city of Jerusalem, for the entertainment of guests.

Emperors, Princes, and Dukes

Rulers in a Confused Europe

The end of the Middle Ages constituted an era of war, disaster, and civil strife, not only in France, but throughout Europe. Italy fell in anarchy, civil war raged in Spain, England suffered revolts and feuds among the nobility, while starvation and plague raged everywhere. Tensions increased along the borders of Europe. In Russia, the Mongols abolished the existing power structure. In the southeast, the Turks did the same. They would only conquer Constantinople in 1453 but by then they would occupy large areas of the Balkans.

In England and France, royal power did not substantially decrease despite the universal chaos and misery because the authority of the king in each case was no longer in question. Before the formation of centralized monarchic governments, vassals had tried incessantly to improve their own positions at the expense of the sovereign. Over the course of the Middle Ages, this changed,

Tomb effigy of Ottokar II, ruler of Bohemia (1253–1278), in the Cathedral of Prague

with the nobles preferring to support the king. Where the ruler was very young or weak, they would take control of royal power, frequently through regents. Once a particular political crisis ended, both king and nobles would benefit from the reinforced royal power structure.

The possibility of the universal domination of Europe by the Holy Roman Empire once appeared feasible. However, control of both the German and Italian parts of the empire had proven too high an aim for Frederick I Barbarossa (1152–1190). Frederick II (1220–1250) understood that he could succeed only by concentrating on Italy. It was impossible to predict how imperial policy would evolve in the future because of the dynastic changes in Germany, but it was evident that the power of the vassals in choosing a king had increased.

The Great Interregnum
In the thirteenth century, the Holy Roman Empire seemed doomed to disappear with the Hohenstaufens. The autonomy of the German princes had heightened, while the attention of Frederick II was focused on Italy. The confusion that resulted from his sudden death in 1250 had only increased their influence. They were well aware that it would be unwise to jeopardize their position by choosing another emperor as flamboyant as Frederick I Barbarossa.

As a result, for the period of twenty years known as the Great Interregnum (1254–1273), there was no generally recognized liege lord in the empire. Whatever was left of imperial power faded quickly over this time. The German Empire became a patchwork quilt made up of small states. It would remain like this for centuries.

States varied in size from small countries to large principalities. These states varied greatly in prestige and power, as well. In the center of the empire was a collection of small counties: Nassau, Katzenellnbogen, Waldeck, and Lippe. In general, these did not consist of contiguous territory. Unified states with defined, all-encompassing borders were just developing. A ruler could hold scattered properties and have jurisdiction in some places, while other parts of the countryside might still be controlled by local nobility.

Genuine territorial kingdoms were estab-

Portrait of Rudolf I Habsburg, who lived from 1218 to 1291. He defeated Ottokar of Bohemia and changed the traditional policy of the emperors by keeping the conquered territories to himself.

Miniature from 1497 showing the harbor of Hamburg. Hamburg was a member of the Hanseatic League, an influential coalition of merchants and traders from cities in western and northern Europe.

1389

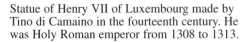
Statue of Henry VII of Luxembourg made by Tino di Camaino in the fourteenth century. He was Holy Roman emperor from 1308 to 1313.

others. To the south were the large territories of Bavaria, Bohemia, Saxony, Swabia, and Austria.

Several interesting institutional developments occurred in the patchwork quilt. The Swiss *Eidgenossenschaft* (Confederation) is probably the best known. Switzerland was formally part of the German Empire. It consisted of a number of isolated and independent communities of farmers who had settled in various valleys. In 1291, three of these communities, Uri, Schwyz, and Unterwalden, united to form an "Everlasting Union." They created an organizational structure where internal autonomy was combined with external cooperation. Lucerne joined in 1332, Zurich in 1351, Glarus and Zug in 1352, Bern in 1353. The peace treaty between the Swiss League and the Hapsburgs took place in 1352. In 1481 Fribourg and Solothurn were admitted into the confederation. The war with the Swabian League that began in 1499 ended with the Peace of Basel in 1501, the same year in which Basel and Schaffhausen joined the Swiss Confederation, which included Appenzell in 1513.

Each of the regions had its own internal government, and there was no constitution, no common officers, law courts, or standardized coinage. The confederation was based on an oath of mutual aid and assistance against aggressors. This was formalized in 1481, with the stipulation that the oath be renewed every five years, and that the states would agree to avoid fomenting discord in other states.

Another development was the Swabian League of Cities. In 1331, there was a union of twenty-two cities under the protection of Louis of Bavaria. Between 1367 and 1372 there was a civil war with lesser nobles who were threatened by the cities' power. The cities lost. In 1376 a new league was formed with fourteen cities; they were victorious against the nobility in 1377. Other cities in Swabia, Rhineland, Bavaria, and Fraconia joined. In 1488 Emperor Frederick III met with the Swabian estates and formed the Great Swabian League in which twenty-two cities were represented as one of four equal parties, the others being nobles from each of

lished from the thirteenth century on at the periphery of the empire. In the west, these included the county of Burgundy (referred to as Franche-Comté to distinguish it from the French duchy of Burgundy), Hainault, Brabant, and Holland. North and east lay Brunswick, Pomerania, Brandenburg, and

the three families. It was dissolved under the influence of the Reformation in 1534. Its goals were to protect the ability of the member cities to answer directly to the emperor and not to the lesser nobility.

The Hansa or Hanseatic League of North German cities was a union of free cities that worked actively to promote their own interests in trade, with representatives in London, the Scandinavian countries, and Poland. It was formed in the twelfth century and had considerable power by the middle of the thirteenth century. Lübeck and other Hansa cities colonized other areas along the coast, beyond Scandinavia into Lithuania and as far as Novgorod.

Around a thousand major landowners living usually on small independent estates within the German principalities answered only to the emperor. They were called *Freiherren* (or freemen). Their holding comprised some of the small autonomous entities of the Holy Roman Empire.

After a few decades (1154–1273) without an emperor, tension between regional and local rulers increased. The landowners eventually came to regard the situation as unacceptable. There seemed to be universal agreement that unity had to be restored, preferably with as little central authority as possible.

In 1278, it was decided that the emperor would be appointed by electors. Together, the most prominent princes and archbishops in the empire would choose an emperor who would continue in that capacity for life. In 1314 two emperors were elected, Frederick of Austria (d. 1330) and Louis of Bavaria (d. 1347). In 1330, by the Treaty of Hagnenau, Louis of Bavaria was recognized as Emperor Louis IV by the Hapsburgs. The permanent board of electors, consisting of the archbishops of Mainz, Trier, and Cologne and the kings of Bohemia, Saxony, Brandenburg, and Palatinate, was established by the time of the next election, that of Charles IV of Luxembourg in 1347. This method of succession was intended to avoid the risk of establishing a powerful imperial dynasty.

The first "new style" emperor was the little-known Rudolf of Hapsburg. He owned land and a castle on the upper Rhine and had a reputation of compliant behavior. It was said that he could never accomplish anything on his own. Hence, he was considered an excellent choice for emperor by autonomy-minded vassals. Rudolf (who reigned from 1273 to 1291) seemed well aware of his reputation and, at first, did nothing to alter it. He never attempted to outshine his vassals. He preferred to stay in his family castle and function like a referee, though he regularly organized wars against raiding knights.

Portrait of Emperor Charles IV, who reigned from 1346 to 1378

Seal of Emperor Charles IV

In 1276 Rudolf made his move. Bohemia was ruled by King Ottokar, a vassal to the German emperor who conquered the principalities of Austria, Styria, and Carinthia. When Ottokar appeared indifferent to the weaker emperor, Rudolf relieved him of all these possessions except Bohemia. With the help of a number of other kings who disapproved of the Bohemian expansion, Ottokar

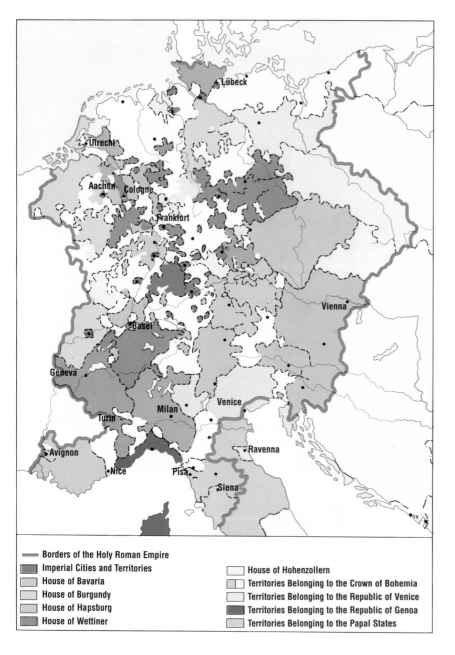

The Holy Roman Empire in the Middle of the Fifteenth Century

Legend:
- Borders of the Holy Roman Empire
- Imperial Cities and Territories
- House of Bavaria
- House of Burgundy
- House of Hapsburg
- House of Wettiner
- House of Hohenzollern
- Territories Belonging to the Crown of Bohemia
- Territories Belonging to the Republic of Venice
- Territories Belonging to the Republic of Genoa
- Territories Belonging to the Papal States

was defeated.

According to tradition, Rudolf should have rewarded his helpers by offering them the confiscated land, but he did not. Ruling Austria, Styria, and Carinthia on his own, he became a powerful emperor, earning the respect of the electors. Rudolf made decisions that would influence imperial policies for centuries to come, such as consolidating the territories of the empire and renouncing

imperial claims in Lombardy and Sicily. (After his death in 1291, however, the regents did not elect another Hapsburg emperor. They installed the weakling Adolf of Nassau on the throne.)

Every new emperor tried to use his imperial title to obtain as much new territory as possible by incorporating lapsed fiefs. Nonetheless, the emperor's role was still considered essential, and the post was respected. The emperor was still considered to be the major secular power in charge of defending Christianity against the infidel, the Muslims. He was also expected to maintain order in the Christian world. It was on imperial authority that the Council of Constance had been convened in an effort to restore unity within the Latin-Christian world.

During the course of the fourteenth century, the concept of the empire slowly took on a more restrictive and Germanic meaning. The emperor came to embody the increasing nationalist feelings. The Holy Roman Empire changed its name to the Holy Roman Empire of the German Nation. It was evident by now that whoever was elected to rule Germany would automatically become the Holy Roman emperor. The position no longer required papal consent or coronation.

But to some degree this imperial orientation toward Germany weakened the office of emperor in the eyes of the rest of the world. In the Italian part of the empire, the emperor was increasingly regarded as a stranger, possibly because emperors visited there less often. Elsewhere in Europe, where kings were reinforcing their individual positions, the universality of the imperial was a problem. A motto that gained currency in France said, "The king is emperor of his own kingdom." In Spain it was argued that, while the rest of the empire might have fallen into the hands of the Germans, Spain had not.

There was a great deal of confusion between the concept of an empire and its practical execution. Rudolf of Hapsburg used the title of emperor to strengthen his own position, but it did not help his family's hold on the throne. An array of families ascended the throne, generally ruling in a mediocre fashion.

During the fourteenth and fifteenth centuries, the German principalities established rudimentary central governments, usually consisting of special departments to administer justice and to regulate finances within a feudal council.

Estate meetings were also of great importance. These were held by the landowners, who invited representatives of the three classes: nobility, clergy, and commoners.

Initially the meetings played a modest role, but they grew more important over time. Most of the German National Domain was formed by small rulers usurping the emperor's rights. They depended on their subjects to stabilize and legitimize their positions—and to finance their political aspirations. This had become clear in the estate meetings. As a result, the meeting agendas and regulations became more specific. On territorial matters, they ruled there would be no more land theft and no foreigners would serve as council members. On matters regarding their own institutions, they decided on the frequency and composition of the meetings. On foreign policy matters they considered peace negotiations and made decisions regarding dynasties and marriages.

In 1440, the electors again elected a scion of the Hapsburg family to become emperor. It was the rather spineless Frederick III, who was mainly interested in birds. Though he spent as little time as possible governing his lands, his motto spoke of far-reaching interests: AEIOU, *Alles Erdreich ist Österreich Untertan* (the entire world belongs to Austria). The motto indicated the next step, nationalism, even if the bird-breeding emperor was not interested in taking it. Nevertheless, Frederick managed to betroth his son Maximilian to Mary, heiress to Burgundy. Frederick III would become the great-great-grandfather of Charles V, the most powerful king of the sixteenth century, emperor of the Holy Roman Empire of the German Nation, king of Spain, and ruler of the Netherlands.

A New Type of Ruler in Italy

For Italy, the Hohenstaufen period also signaled a change in direction, producing even

Portrait of Emperor Henry VII painted by Andrea di Bonaiuto. Between 1310 and 1313 this emperor led several military campaigns in Italy, hoping to regain authority for the imperial crown in these territories.

1393

Picture from the fifteenth century depicting a fight between two armed groups. During the fourteenth and fifteenth centuries Italy was tormented by constant armed conflicts between the Guelphs (party of the pope) and the Ghibellines (party of the emperor).

greater fragmentation that existed in the past. The dichotomy between the north and the south of Italy intensified. The south consisted of the kingdoms of Naples and Sicily. Both were tied to the kingdom of Aragon by personal union. Both kingdoms had been able to maintain the strongly centralized bureaucratic government created earlier by Frederick II.

The political situation in northern Italy, which included the papal states, had never been more confusing. During the fourteenth century, the German emperors had repeatedly attempted to regain their power in the Italian part of the realm. Even when they acknowledged their ties with the Church by traveling to Rome to receive the honors of office from the pope, they were not actually able to exercise authority in Italy. As long as they resided on the Italian Peninsula, they could occasionally make political statements, but as soon as they returned to

Germany, Italian politics would go its own way.

Politics and social feuds within and among cities as well as between urban and rural areas arose. When the power of the emperor finally ceased to exist, the autonomous cities seized the opportunity to resolve their conflicts. The Italian cities were not only torn within, they were at war with each other. Noble families rose to power and continued to feud in areas, as well. Alliances of feuding parties took on the names of Guelph and Ghibelline, as though reverting to the ancient family feuds.

Papal authority also declined. Pope Boniface VIII favored tax exemption for the French church, not only as a matter of principle but because it would mean more revenues, which were needed to fight feuding noble families like the Orsinis and the Colonnas.

With lack of central authority allowing

the city of Pisa was defeated and became subjected to Florentine authority in 1409, and didn't regain independence until 1494.

City expansion was also occurring in the papal states. Cities like Bologna, Ferrara, and Perugia were independent to a large degree and able to add major portions of the countryside to their territories.

Consequently, the countryside was divided among the various cities. Their borders were a constant source of contention, providing ample reason to draw swords, which was not normally a specialty for Italian officials, traditionally business owners, merchants, and bankers. They were also tradesmen and artisans and an ever-growing number of paupers, none trained for battle either. The cities,

each city to seize and control the surrounding countryside, the cities became small states, a development most noticeable in the Po Valley and in Tuscany.

Milan had been the dominant city in the Po Valley since the middle of the eleventh century, although during the late Middle Ages the city of Venice had slowly started to show interest in the mainland. Milan recognized Venice's ascendancy over cities such as Verona and Padua, but still considered Venice's traditional political role to be geared toward keeping control of the trade routes in the eastern basin of the Mediterranean. In the no-man's land between these two superpowers, Milan and Venice, the city of Mantua was able to develop as a principality.

During the late thirteenth to the fifteenth centuries, the city of Florence in Tuscany rose to the position of undisputed leader, at great military expense. After a tough battle,

therefore, generally employed *condottieri* (mercenaries), who were paid to go to war. Their fees increased with each victory.

The life of a condottieri was exciting and dangerous. He could not afford to disappoint his principals, knowing that the opposing party would use every trick to eliminate him. The mercenary did not fit into any existing social category. He did not derive his power from a feudal estate, he was not an urban aristocrat, he was not a priest. He was his own man, not really part of any community. His success made him rich and feared, but if he failed, he lost everything. Personal success was all that mattered to him.

Condottieri eventually became interested

The harbor of Genoa. During the fourteenth century Genoa was one of the most important trading cities in Italy

In this miniature, Marco Polo leaves on the journey that would take him to China. Also seen is the harbor of Venice, one of the largest trading cities in medieval Italy.

in intervening in urban disputes. Their foremost weapon was terror. Some of them worked their way up to becoming the city dictators who ruled most Italian cities by keeping feuding parties out of each others' way and maintaining their own positions of authority. They were frequently supported by the local citizenry, who were happy to keep out of the battles. Generally they came to power by means of a coup d'état, earning their positions by violence rather than traditional law. Their power rarely survived them. Upon passing of its condottieri, a city often returned to its old state of chaos, subject to the feuds of the Guelphs and Ghibellines, until the next condottieri took control.

Mercenaries were notorious for their misconduct. At the end of the fifteenth century, a man by the name of Boccalino conquered the papal city of Osimo. He believed it would be very profitable for the city to sur-

render to the Turks, which might have taken place if the banker-dictator of Florence did not change Boccalino's mind by bribing him with huge amounts of gold.

Milan

Milan was an important city in late antiquity, and rose again in the ninth century. Milan gained wealth through trade. Each of the north's major cities—Milan, Venice, Florence, Siena, Genoa, Pisa—gained control of smaller cities nearby and dominated the region, largely through the aggressive *podestàs* and condottieri who had gained power. Compared to other cities, Milan was rather stable. The Viscontis ruling it were exposed to wars, uprisings, and shifts of power and yet were able to maintain control. The first Visconti in power was Otto, archbishop of Milan, in 1262. The Viscontis led until the death of Filippo in 1477. Though some were patrons of the arts, all the Viscontis were said to be despots. A good example was Bernabò Visconti, who came to power in 1354. The people of Milan were ordered to care for his 5,000 hounds because Bernabò enjoyed hunting. He was also said to enjoy increasing taxes and torturing people.

Bernabò was deposed and probably murdered in 1385. Gian Galeazzo Visconti, a nephew, objected to Bernabò's giving away their mutually owned inheritance as dowries to the important families into which his daughters married. Gian Galeazzo's honest leadership was welcomed by the citizens of Milan when his forces took over the city. He also ruled Lombardy. (One of the few structures of this period is the Duomo or Cathedral of Milan, built on Galeazzo's orders.)

When Gian Galeazzo died in 1403, the

Portrait of Bianca Marie, the daughter of Filippo Maria Visconti and wife of Francesco Sforza

Portrait of Francesco Sforza, duke of Milan from 1401 to 1466. He was the leader of one of the best-trained armies of mercenaries. He married Bianca Marie, daughter of the previous duke of Milan.

realm of the Viscontis fell apart. His son, Giovanni Maria, was able to hold on to Milan, ordering anyone in the streets who cried "peace" to be killed. Even the celebration of the mass had to be altered to accommodate this eccentricity. Giovanni Maria was not able to hold out in Milan for long,

Portrait of Filippo Maria Visconti, duke of Milan until 1447

though, in spite of his tyrannical rule. Conspirators killed him in front of a church.

Yet the soldiers supported his heir, Filippo Maria, thus keeping Milan in the hands of the same family of tyrants. Filippo Maria was a rational man. He controlled his realm effectively, without ever showing himself to the outside world. He lived in a beautiful palace where he felt safe, surrounded by extensive gardens where everyone spied on everyone else.

The Visconti family died out with Filippo

Maria. His son-in-law, Francesco Sforza, duke of Milan, took over in 1450. In contrast to his in-laws, he was popular and not tyrannical. This was, to a lesser extent, also true for his successors. Some of them, although dictators, were benevolent patriarchs. Federigo de Montefeltro, lord of Urbino, duke of Milan, was a friendly book lover who despised gambling and wasting money. Known as a patron of the arts, he turned Urbino into the foremost center of arts and literature, with his palace as a showplace. The citizens benefited from his just rule, and Federigo could walk around the city without bodyguards. He was, however, an exception; in general, Italy was in the grip of tyrants.

Toward the end of the fifteenth century, other outside powers became involved with Italy. The French king Charles VIII invaded Italy in 1493, ultimately marching into Naples to claim his throne in 1495. Papal forces drove him back to France later that year. This was the beginning of a confused and disastrous period. Italy became embroiled in disputes between the Valois family of France and the House of Hapsburg, which was at first German, but from the sixteenth century on, was also of Spain. Italian alliances switched back and forth from one superpower to the other.

This period ended with permanent Spanish hegemony in the south of Italy and the western Po Valley, including Milan. Tuscany and a few smaller principalities in the north ended up on the side of the French. Genoa and Venice were able to negotiate some measure of neutrality, while Lombardy became famous for its numerous razed cities.

Central Europe During the Middle Ages

Poland, Scandinavia, and the Order of Teutonic Knights

During the late Middle Ages, Denmark, Sweden, and Norway were separate kingdoms, occasionally united under one king. The first Christian king, Olaf the Holy (Olaf of Norway), was on the throne from 1015–1030. His rudimentary efforts at conversion formed the foundation on which King Canute the Great, king of Denmark from 1014 who killed Olaf in battle, became ruler of Norway and built a Christian kingdom. While Scandinavia was ruled by his successors, it remained at least nominally Christian, with all the attributes of its neighbors in the south, including churches and bishops. Scandinavia covered a vast, wild, sparsely populated area. By the eleventh century, the major population centers in Scandinavia were well established and the three present-day states of Sweden, Norway, and Denmark gradually emerged.

Consolidation
Norway
While the Swedes and the Danes focused their attention on the Baltic Sea, the Norwegians explored the Atlantic. Since the early Middle Ages the Norwegians had explored the northern seas. Now they battled to hold on to the ocean regions and the

1399

The Castle of Elsinore in Denmark, strategically situated along a sea trade route

islands they had once dominated without opposition. In the fifth century various north-central European tribes established kingdoms in the British Isles, and in the ninth century Norse and Danish tribes established powerful kingdoms in England. The Norwegians exported fish to the British and imported grain. They launched military expeditions to safeguard their dominion over the Orkneys, the Shetland Islands, the Faeroe Islands, and the Hebrides. They repeatedly threatened Ireland and Scotland.

In 1266 the Hebrides and the Isle of Man were ceded to Scotland by Magnus VI in return for recognition of the Norwegian claim to the Orkney and Shetland Islands. In about 1260, the Norwegian Empire found its furthest outreaches when Iceland acknowledged the Norwegian king. Iceland desperately needed Norwegian grain and wood and the products made by its craftsmen. In turn, Iceland provided Norway with fish and the products of its local farming and stock breeding.

In Norway, King Haakon IV (reigned 1217–1263) and Magnus the Lawmender

(reigned 1263–1280) restored their realm at home and overseas. Magnus created the first national code of laws in Europe, and in 1278 allowed German merchants to stay in Norway through the summer. A blockade in 1294 forced his son Eric II (1280–1299) to effectively allow them to monopolize trade south of Bergen, while Norwegians had control of Iceland and Greenland. The period from the thirteenth to the fourteenth centuries was characterized by more domestic wars. It was not until years later that Norway regained a measure of stability. Trade was still dominated by the Hanseatic League.

The political unification of Iceland and Norway, who were effectively united in the thirteenth century, did not take place until 1944, when the Icelanders gained their independence from Denmark. They had come under Danish control as a result of the Union of Kalmar (1397), with Margaret of Denmark, Queen of Norway, Denmark, and Sweden, ruling even though Eric of Pomerania (1412–1434) was king.

Denmark
In the middle of the fourteenth century, the Scandinavian states were consolidated under one king, but the union was superficial at best. In Denmark, the royal power was destroyed as a result of the dominance of the

More than 400 years before Columbus, the Norwegians landed in North America. This is a statue (in St. Paul, Minnesota) honoring Leif Eriksson. He was the first to sail along the coast of Labrador.

bishops and a shortage of funds at court. In 1282, the king was forced to convene the Danehof, an annual meeting of noblemen, prelates, and dignitaries with legislative power. The Danehof's decisions were eventually overshadowed by church councils (the last Danehof met in 1413). Conflict among the clergy, the nobility, and the crown tore the country apart. It was sometimes without a head of state, and foreign powers were often able to exert an influence.

Sweden

From the year 1250 on, beginning with Valdemar (died 1275), Sweden was ruled by the Foljungar dynasty, which founded Stockholm and stimulated economic development. Earlier, in the twelfth century, many German merchants immigrated to centers such as Copenhagen and Lubeck, and there were sizeable colonies of German merchant families in these areas. The Swedes had

Etching made in 1581 of Bergen, the most important Norwegian trade city and an outpost of the Hanseatic League at that time

begun trading fish, timber, walrus, ivory, and fur with the Germans.

German merchants from Lübeck, the major Hanseatic base in the Baltic, were exempted from Swedish customs duties in the twelfth century, and by 1225 they had established the "Community of German visitors" in the trade center of Visby. The Hansa merchants grew more and more unpopular, ultimately controlling another major trading center, which was conquered first by Sweden, then by Denmark. The alliance of the Scandinavian kings against the Hansa resulted in a series of battles, concluding

with the Treaty of Stralsund in 1370, which restored revenues and castles to the Hansa.

Poland

The Polish kingdom emerged in the eleventh century as a formidable Slavic realm. The German merchants who formed the Hanseatic League established settlements from the twelfth century. With the advance eastward of the Germans who were robbing the Slavs of their land, they were forced into battle. The Germans took over Pomerania and Silesia while Polish princes were battling each other for control of Kraków (Cracow). In the thirteenth century, Poland was divided and teeming with Germans. Favorable terms for immigrants encouraged settlement of new towns by free peasants from Germany and the Netherlands, as well as the Jews. Attempts at unification failed as a result of resistance put up by the immigrants and the kings of Hungary and Bohemia. It was not until the fourteenth century that King Wladislaw IV (reigned 1306–1333), with the support of the noblemen, managed to force his German citizens into submission. However, he was forced to accept the loss of much of his land to the

The twelfth-century wall of the city of Visby on the Swedish island of Gotland is one of Europe's best preserved medieval fortifications. During the twelfth to fourteenth centuries Visby was an important trade center.

German merchants, the king of Bohemia, and the grand master of the Order of Teutonic Knights.

Order of Teutonic Knights

A new power in the Baltic, the Order of Teutonic Knights, was founded in 1198, emerging from the German branch of the Knights Hospitalers (Order of St. John). The knights had set out to Christianize Palestine, later turning their attention to the pagans of the Baltic and taking over territories by military force after it was clear that Palestine was lost. Invited into Poland in 1226 to settle internal conflicts and to unite the kingdom, within a hundred years they controlled much of the Baltic Coast. In the course of the thirteenth century, another formidable enemy appeared on the scene. Like the Huns eight hundred years earlier, the Mongols discovered the lowland plain of the European peninsula. They overturned the great Russian kingdoms in a single massive assault and reached the first settlements of German colonists in the 1240s. Novgorod was situated considerably to the south of what is now the city of Leningrad. During the thirteenth century, it was a powerful merchant city that chose as its motto "No one can stand against God and Novgorod." The city's king, Alexander Nevsky (reigned 1236–1263) had confirmed the truth of this motto by annihilating an army of German soldiers at the Neva. However, he did not dare to send out his troops against the Mongols. Finally, laborious negotiations resulted in a humiliating treaty, under which the powerful merchant city owed tribute to the Mongolian rulers.

Nevertheless, the Poles and the Germans assembled an army to engage in desperate battle against the Mongols in 1241, during

Part of a Flemish tapestry
that was ordered by King Sigismund II
of Poland in the second half of the
sixteenth century

Colored pen drawing
from c.1440 depicting the
loading of a *kog*, a type
of ship characteristically used
by Hanseatic merchants

the battle of Liegnitz. In spite of the courage of the knights from the West, they were defeated. Still the resistance was a success: The Mongols won the battle, but paid for their victory with great loss of life, including their leader, Ughetai. They were unable to advance and returned to the vast Russian plain. Their offensive was stopped at Liegnitz.

The imperial power north of the Alps was severely threatened. Frederick II did not take the threat seriously at first and responded arrogantly to the Mongol ultimatums. After the defeat of the Teutonic Knights, the death of the duke of Silesia, and the Mongol conquests in Hungary, however, he appealed to other western rulers to join a united defense against them. Pope Innocent IV also called for a crusade against the Mongols.

The Mongols settled in the middle and lower reaches of the Volga. After costly attacks on Hungary and Poland, Batu, grandson of Ghengis Khan, built his residence in Sarai, where he founded an independent state, the Khanate of the Golden Horde, that would remain in existence for many centuries. All the Russian kings continued to be subject to the Mongols, under even more humiliating conditions than under Alexander Nevsky. In Novgorod, the Hanseatic merchants owned the trading monopoly and managed the export trade.

The kingdom of Sweden ❯
flourished after the year 1250.
The building of the
Cathedral of Stockholm,
begun in 1306, was a sign of
Sweden's economic
prosperity.

The Hanseatic League

In the thirteenth century, a new concept appeared at the time when trade was on the rise in a region with little experience in central rule. Called the hanseatic concept, it originated in the organizations of merchants called *hansas* (groups), caravans formed to travel jointly through dangerous territory to annual markets. These hansas of merchants were well organized and able to defend themselves. In the course of time, the hanseatic leagues evolved into permanent associations, originally regional in nature. In France, a community *(universitas)* of Italian merchants had been founded, regulating

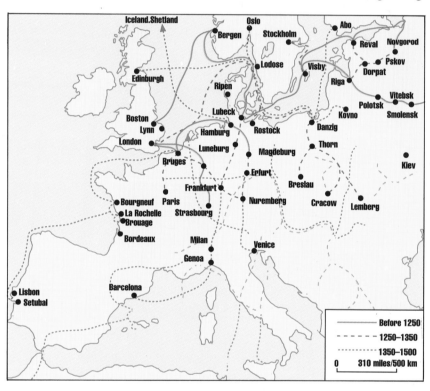

The main trade routes and cities of the Hanseatic League

their activities and practices and determining who could belong. The Provençals had a similar organization.

The hansa concept gained broader meaning, eventually connoting no longer a union of merchants, but a union of cities. During the thirteenth century, the Hanseatic League emerged as a powerful federation that played a role in political affairs as well as trade. The number of members continued to grow until the fifteenth century when more than a hundred cities belonged.

The advantages of membership were evident. The Hanseatic League had trading posts in London, Bergen, Bruges, and the Russian city of Novgorod. Time after time, members were forbidden to teach nonmembers Russian. Ships belonging to the Hanseatic cities hunted down smugglers who engaged in illegal trade out of small harbors. More than once, drastic measures such as

New Monastic Orders: Monks with Swords

As a result of the crusades, a new form of monastic life developed: new orders emerged that did not seek solitude and sobriety, but wished to defend their faith with swords in their hands. This was no surprising development, for the crusader states possessed only a small strip of land, and their existence was threatened from the beginning. Still, the orders of knighthood, as they were called very soon, did not start out as military organizations. On the contrary: the first of these orders initially specialized completely in taking care of the poor and the sick.

After the conquest of Jerusalem many pilgrims went to the Holy Land, but many fell ill as a result of the long journey and a very different climate. Even before the First Crusade, Italian merchants founded a hospital for Christians in the Holy Land, but that was not prepared for a sudden flood of sick people. A better organization was needed.

The first who realised this were the friars of St. John's hospital, and they founded the

The Castle of Pontferrada in Spain, a Templar fort

1406

Many rulers founded orders that were similar to the knights' orders. Like the English Order of the Garter, many did not have a religious character. Here Knights of the French Order of the Golden Fleece are seen with King John the Good.

Order of St. John. During the twelfth century, two more orders emerged after this example, the Templars and the Order of German Knights. They soon started to intervene in political and military problems, and together all these orders formed a *militia Christi,* an army for the service of Christ. In the vows that every brother had to take on entering the order, an extra task was included: the defense of the Holy Land against all non-Christians.

At the same time, the sort of people that joined these orders changed: a lot of real knights now signed up, and in the end only knights were allowed to join. The orders built their "monasteries" — in fact imposing castles — on strategic spots in the crusader states. Less and less time was devoted to the care of the sick, but they still received huge amounts of money from Europe to keep up their good work. When the crusader states collapsed, these orders of knighthood could easily survive, for by that time they had plenty money.

The Order of St. John remained faithful to its ideals, but it moved its headquarters to the island of Rhodes, which they stubbornly defended against the Turks until far into the sixteenth century. When they finally had to give up their stronghold, they moved to Malta.

The Templars survived in a comparable way on the island of Cyprus, but their activities in Europe as bankers did not exactly improve their reputation. In 1310 Pope Clemens V dissolved the order, and after this its grand master and several knights were accused of heresy and burned at the stake. Their possessions in France were confiscated by Philip the Fair, the king of that country.

The Order of German Knights soon moved its activities to the frontier between Christians and the faithless in Eastern Europe. Its headquarters were established in Marienburg near Dantzig Gdansk. From there, the German knights organized the conquest of the Slavonic territories, and lots of enthusiastic European noblemen joined their ranks. The result of these campaigns was the formation of the Baltic Empire, which would survive up to the sixteenth century.

armed conflict and a blockade were taken. Northern Europe could be regarded, as a Hanseatic province. The Low German that was spoken in Lübeck was not only the language of merchants, it was also used in the Danish chancery. German merchants migrated to Scandinavia, Poland, and the Baltic coast of the Russian peninsula in the twelfth to fourteenth centuries, setting up powerful merchant colonies that choked out competition.

The Hanseatic League was challenged by two enemies: pirates and the king of Denmark. He controlled the Sont Strait, which is the passage to the Baltic Sea, and demanded a hefty toll from passing ships. This interference by the Hanseatic League created internal conflicts in Denmark and a number of wars. In 1370, under the Treaty of Stralsund, the Hanseatic League obtained an exemption for merchants from member cities. This privilege would be confirmed by the Peace of Vordingborg in 1435, when, after nine years of fighting with the Hansa, Eric of Pomerania gave up his claims to Schlewig and exempted Hansa ships from his tolls.

It was more difficult to cope with the *Vitalienbruder,* pirates who plundered Visby, a German colony on the island of Gotland, Sweden, a major trade center in 1392. In this battle, however, the Hanseatic League received support from the Teutonic Order.

The Teutonic Order ruled Prussia by 1283, and controlled the Baltic coast of Poland by the mid-fourteenth century, including Danzig, or Gdansk. Some of these four hundred settlements developed into trade centers that sought to join the Hanseatic League. The order itself exported the wood, grain, and amber produced.

The Union of Kalmar
The process of unification in northern Europe proceeded slowly and not without difficulty. In 1322, Magnus Erickson was crowned king of both Norway and Sweden, but the two countries split apart soon afterward. A more lasting effect was produced by the king of Denmark, King Waldemar IV Atterdag (elected 1340). His name means "next day," since the king was a procrastinator. He had to endure the humiliation of the

King Gustav I Vasa,
ruler of the kingdom of Sweden
from 1496 to 1560, in a
painting from 1558

Treaty of Stralsund in 1370, a defeat for Scandinavian autonomy. His daughter Margaret, heir to the Danish crown and wife of King Haakon VI of Norway and Sweden (son of Magnus), made the unification a fact. In 1376, she became regent of Denmark. Four years later, she obtained the same position in Norway, on behalf of her son Olaf IV, who was four years old. In Sweden, King Albert of Mecklenburg was fiercely opposed by a group of noblemen. In 1389, with the help of the rebels, Margaret defeated him at the battle of Lonkoping. Sweden recognized her as queen, but Albert continued to offer resistance for another six years. Olaf had died two years before the battle of Lonkoping, and so Margaret remained regent without a successor. She solved this problem by appointing her nephew Eric of Pomerania as heir to the throne.

The three kingdoms held a meeting at Kalmar in 1397 and approved her decree. However, the representatives stipulated that each country should maintain its own institutions. The Union of Kalmar was not viable. The king of Germany and the Danish councilors encountered Swedish opposition, and Sweden remained virtually independent for most of the fifteenth century. Besides, the kings did not succeed in keeping the Hanseatic League at bay. King Eric took the side of the English and Dutch merchants, which led to war with the powerful Germans. He was defeated in 1435. In 1523, Sweden broke away permanently after a long series of civil wars. Norway and Denmark continued to be united until the Congress of Vienna in 1815, when Norway became a part of Sweden. In 1906, it regained its indepen-

Reliquary of Saint Sigismund, donated by Casimir the Great of Poland to the Cathedral of Plock c.1370

From 1309 to 1457 the Knights of the German Order played an important role in the grain trade, from Prussia to Western Europe. This is a nineteenth-century engraving of their stronghold along the Vistula River in Poland.

dence, appointing as its king a young prince from the Danish dynasty.

Unification of Poland and Lithuania

While the unification of Scandinavia came about as a result of the Hanseatic threat, the Treaty of the Teutonic Order caused a similar union between two Slavic nations. Poland gained a measure of stability in the thirteenth century when King Casimir the Great temporarily settled the country's problems with the order and the king of Bohemia. He took up residence in the old city of Krakow, where he founded a famous university. He attempted to make up for the lack of Polish citizens by offering strong protection to Jewish, Greek, and Armenian merchants.

To be able to withstand the German threat, Poland sought an alliance with the kingdom of Hungary. However, this ended in a disaster, because the countries did not have sufficient common interests. The only alternative left the Poles was to join forces with the heathen country of Lithuania, which was constantly threatened by the Teutonic Order and its obsession with the Crusades. The Lithuanians lived in the forests and swamps of the Dvina and Memel Rivers. They had formed a political unit since the middle of the thirteenth century. The dukes of Lithuania built a number of fortresses and took over some small states in western Russia.

In 1385, the queen of Poland (Jadwiga of Anjou, daughter of Louis of Hungary) married Duke Jagiello. The Lithuanian agreed to be baptized and chose the Polish name of Vladislav. While his subjects did not imme-diately accept Christianity and the unification, an immense power block was formed. Vladislav Jagiello supported the Prussians against the Teutonic Knights, and disrupted trade between Prussia and Poland. As a result, the grand master of the order declared war on Poland-Lithuania. The Battle of Tannenberg in 1410 marked the beginning of the knights' decline. It was a horrible disaster in which the grand master of the order and thousands of his knights lost their lives. Poland-Lithuania was victorious. The fortress of Marienberg fell thirty-six years after the battle of Tannenberg.

A supervisor directs serfs in Poland in this woodcut from the sixteenth century

French ceramic plate from the fifteenth century, decorated with the coat of arms of the dukes of Burgundy

Burgundy

A New Major Power

In the fifteenth century, at a time when most kingdoms were recuperating and consolidating after the warfare of the preceding period, a surprising development took place. In the northwestern part of the continent, on the border between France and the German Empire, a royal house appeared that developed into a major power within just three generations. The dynasty extended its influence to the extent that all of Europe had to

deal with it. This was the House of Burgundy.

As early as the thirteenth century, the French monarchs had arranged for each of their younger brothers to govern a large area, individually termed an *apanage*. One such brother in the second half of the fourteenth century was Duke Philip I the Bold, brother of King Charles V of France. His apanage included Burgundy.

The territory of Burgundy was conquered by Caesar in the Gallic Wars, and divided first into the Roman provinces of Lugdunensis and Belgic Gaul, later Upper Germany. In the fourth century Roman power dissolved, and the prosperous country was invaded by Germani tribes. It was finally conquered by the Burgundii, a tribe from Savoy who accepted Christianity and formed the First Kingdom of Burgundy, which at its height converted southeast France and reached as far south as Arles and western Switzerland. It was conquered in 534 by the Franks and partitioned numerous times, but Burgundy survived as a political concept.

Living at the time of the Hundred Years' War, Philip tried to build as strong a position as possible at the French court and at home. Behind the scenes he plotted actively with and against the other members of the royal family. He made Burgundy so powerful it became a virtually independent estate. Through marriage to Margaret of Flanders, the heiress of the count of Flanders, he added that county to his possessions. He took possession of Nevers and Franche-Comté by virtue of being brother to the king of France.

Philip was by no means a loyal Valois, the ruling dynasty of France at this period. Although he always considered himself a French prince, he never hesitated to work with the English if it suited him. He was essentially a politician who felt himself part of the court in Paris.

His son, John the Fearless (reigned 1404–1419), was power-hungry. He fought primarily with his cousin, Louis, duke of Orléans, who became regent of France when his brother, King Charles VI, became insane and was no longer able to rule. John plotted against Charles and Louis and is thought to be responsible for the murder of Louis of Orléans in 1407.

John the Fearless was stabbed to death on the Dijon Bridge by Armagnacs loyal to the memory of the murdered Louis of Orléans. His son, Philip III the Good, succeeded him. He continued his father's policies, supporting Henry V of England on the French throne. But in the meantime, Charles VII and the Armagnacs were prospering. The English and the Burgundians were put on the defensive. Philip decided to abandon his allies. By the Treaty of Arras he withdrew from the fighting. In return, Charles had to give up his rights as lord of Flanders and Burgundy, Philip's hereditary counties.

The Burgundian Dream

The duke, meanwhile, had developed ideas about his position that were completely different from those of John the Fearless or Philip the Bold. He wanted an empire of his own, situated between France and Germany. He thought of the piece of the Carolingian Empire that had gone to Lothar some six hundred years earlier, with the breakup of the empire, and devoted himself to achieving this objective.

Philip, nicknamed the "Good," was a capable ruler who knew how to run a duchy. He established order over Flanders and Burgundy. He supported the aristocracy and the merchants in the countryside and in the cities who needed a stable environment and a quiet market for their affairs.

Philip's expansionist policy was most successful in the Netherlands, where he faced a minimum of opposition. The country was divided into a series of feudal kingdoms, each torn by civil conflict within the aristoc-

Effigy of Philip III
the Good

Sword that once belonged to
an infantry soldier of the
Burgundians

racy. Philip originally focused his attention on Holland, which was linked by personal ties with Zeeland and Hainault. He had a claim to the title of count because of his lineage, and his uncle, William of Bavaria, had died without a male heir but left a daughter, Jacoba of Bavaria. The other faction, supported by a majority of the town councils, called for Philip. The duke of Burgundy would only take up the sword if it was absolutely necessary. He was amenable to all kinds of compromises, appointing straw men and conspiring to reach his goal.

In 1425 Jacoba was finally obliged to relinquish her rights to Holland, Zeeland, and Hainault. Within two decades, Philip also added Brabant, Limburg, Namur, and Luxembourg to his realm. He also managed to influence the appointments of bishops in Utrecht and Liège, so that both of these church-states were governed by bishops favoring Burgundy. Within a short time, the Burgundians ruled present-day Belgium and much of what is now Holland.

John the Fearless, duke of Burgundy, receives a book as a gift during an audience at court

The Plague in Europe

About 1440, an outbreak of bubonic plague reached Europe via the rats carried by merchant ships from the Far East. The disease, known for some 3,000 years, occurred in several pandemics that destroyed entire urban populations in the Middle Ages. It has occurred (and still does) in Asia, Africa, the Pacific Islands, Australia, and the Americas. It reached San Francisco in 1900 but was otherwise rare in the United States. Its first European victims were the rich Italian merchant towns like Venice and Florence. No one knew until 1894 that the bubonic plague was caused by bacteria, *Yersina pestis*, that affects both rodents and humans. It is spread by several insects (especially the rat flea *Xenopsylla cheopis*) that normally feed on rat blood but turn to humans when the rats die off in an epidemic. Improved sanitation, large-scale killing of rats, and prevention of their transport in ships from contaminated areas can keep it in check. In humans, the disease takes three forms. Bubonic plague (fatal in four days in 30 to 75 percent of untreated cases) is characterized by enlarged, inflamed lymph nodes, called buboes, in the groin, armpit, or neck. Pneumonic plague (fatal in two or three days in 95 percent of untreated cases) infects the lungs. It is air-

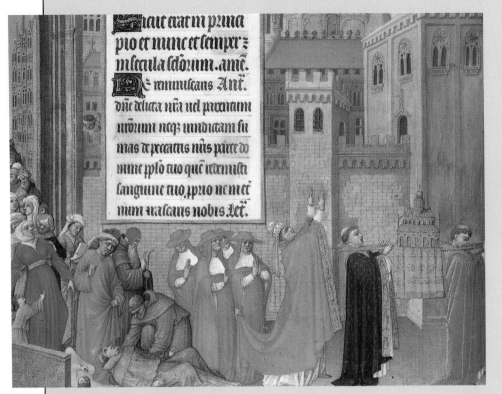

In a fifteenth-century *Book of Hours* the pope Gregory (I) the Great is pictured leading a procession in Rome during a new outbreak of the plague

During the period of the Black Death, groups of flagellants traveled through Europe, trying in this way to ward off the disease. Miniature from the fourteenth century.

borne, transmitted through expectoration by people with the disease. If it spreads to the blood, it is called septicemic plague and is almost invariably fatal, often the same day infection occurs. Septicemic plague can also be transmitted by contact with contaminated food or the hands or objects that have touched the diseased. All victims turn deep purple in color in their last hours, due to respiratory failure; hence, the name *Black Death*. The plague was cured by the use of sulfa drugs during World War II. Today streptomycin and tetracycline are used. Europe panicked since there was no cure in the Middle Ages. Many people thought the plague was divine punishment and did penance in processions of sometimes over a thousand people, walking the city streets. Other people went on pilgrimages, until that was forbidden by the authorities in an effort to stop the epidemic. Flagellants wandered barefoot, dressed in penitential garb, whipping each other and singing hymns. Some flagellants joined movements condemned as heretical by the pope. Some were executed. Others tried to start rebellions. Many people accused the Church of profiting from the inheritances left to it by the dying. The Jews were accused of having caused the epidemic by poisoning the public wells and some were murdered. Trade was nearly put at a standstill. No European city was spared. In Siena the building of the cathedral was interrupted; it has never been completed. The hysteria only died down when the epidemic did. After it ended, a third of the European population had died.

Altarpiece from Germany (fifteenth century), which suggests that the plague was a sign of God's wrath

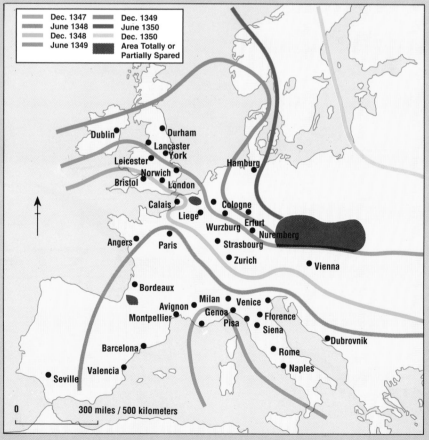

The Course of the Black Death during the fourteenth century

King Charles VII of France and his counselors. Miniature from the fifteenth century.

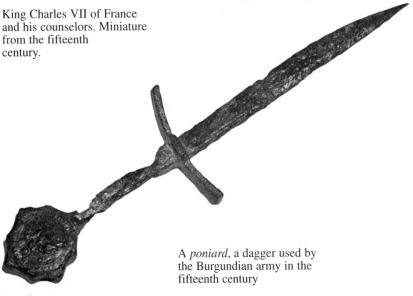

A *poniard*, a dagger used by the Burgundian army in the fifteenth century

Philip the Good kept a magnificent court in his capital at Dijon, characterized by the same flamboyance as the court of Philip the Bold who had once served a pie containing a complete orchestra. Fountains spouted wine on feast days for the public gathered at the palace gates. The Burgundian women set the style in both fashion and good manners throughout Europe, and Burgundy was established as a cultural center. The affluence of the Burgundians had increased in proportion to their territories.

The duke's fondest wish, however, was for a royal crown. He wanted to be on an equal footing with the rulers of Paris and London, but he never succeeded. There were only two people who could grant Philip the Good a crown: the pope in Rome and the emperor of

Church in Burgundy, built in the thirteenth-fifteenth centuries. Its facades are decorated with many different gargoyles.

Germany. Neither had any interest in his coronation. The pope could not afford to alienate the French king, who viewed the rising Burgundian power as a menace. Despite his financial problems, the king was a more powerful friend of the Church than Philip. Withholding the crown from Philip could never bring the papacy into actual conflict with Dijon, but granting it might offend the king.

It was not in the emperor's interest, as

A money changer and his wife, painted by Quentin Massys at the end of the fifteenth century. Among the coins on the table are French ecus, Arabian dinars, and Venetian ducats.

well, to increase his vassal's power. The emperor of Germany remained his liege lord in the Netherlands, and Franche-Comté (or "free Duchy") in eastern Burgundy was a fiefdom of the German Empire.

The result was that Philip held a medium-sized empire that was strategically situated to be either a powerful ally or a powerful enemy. It covered a little less than half the previous territory of the empire of the Carolingian Lothar. Philip's heir, Charles, inherited an extremely well-run estate, Burgundy and the Lowlands. The treasury was full, the subjects were not unhappy, and his authority was generally recognized, but the realm was not unified. The prudent Philip had never tried to forge his various

Assemblies of the Three Orders

Although popular assemblies were held under the feudal system, important political and juridical matters were discussed in meetings of the feudal court. Vassals were obliged to advise their feudal lords during these gatherings.

The rise of the cities complicated this practice. When a ruler granted a city independence, its citizens were automatically exempted from feudal obligations. Yet the cities gained increasing political importance. They also had money, something most medieval rulers lacked. Rulers began to recognize the value of involving cities in government and saw advantages in mutual cooperation. Monarchs began to ask for financial contributions for the costs of government. This required that they allow citizen participation in ruling the country, but it proved to be impossible to involve every citizen in that process. A system of representation was developed to make it possible for a few representatives to speak for a whole city.

The representatives to an assembly were chosen from three groups (or orders): the nobility, the Church, and the urban citizens. (Peasants were not invited.) At first the cities had little influence and felt flattered to be invited at all. This situation would change, but circumstances varied in very country.

England had an active assembly of the three orders, called Parliament, in the thirteenth century. It attempted to supervise the king, and its most important members were the barons. The king, in his turn, tried to limit the assembly's power, but its importance grew over the Hundred Years' War. Eventually the assembly became so powerful it could depose kings, as was the case with Richard II in 1399.

In France, the assembly, called States-General (Etats-Généraux), had never had much power. Around 1300 Philip the Fair

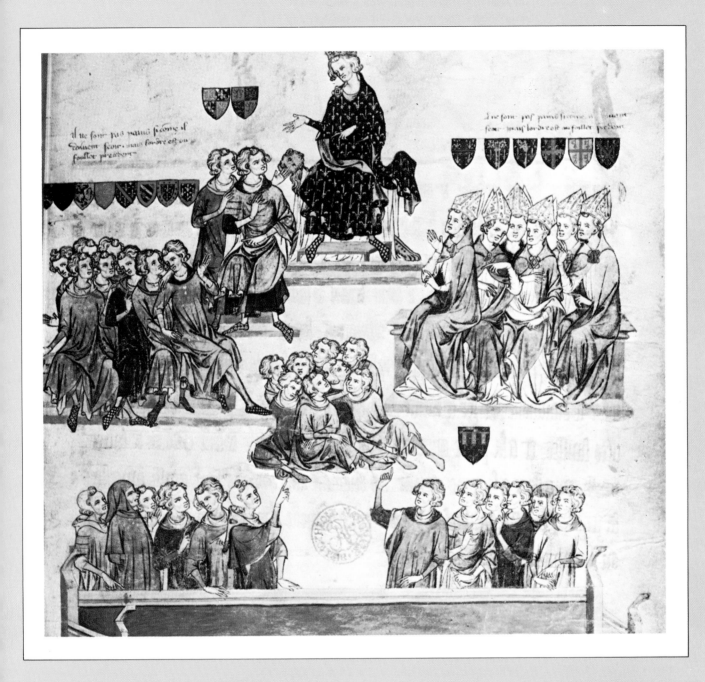

called a meeting of the three orders, prompted only by a lack of money. The kings who came after him tried to avoid such assemblies in order to keep their political actions independent of citizen control.

In the German Empire it was extremely difficult to establish a central assembly of the three orders. The dukes and counts already had effective power and no wish to share it with an urban elite. By the fourteenth century, however, assemblies of the three orders were created that set down rules of behavior for royalty.

French illustration from the fourteenth century depicting Philip VI of Valois supervising an assembly of the States-General

duchies into a single unit, which would have risked their enmity. He left their borders and laws alone and did not curtail duchy privileges. He did, however, make sure that he and his servants held all key positions.

There was only one organization involving all of Philip's counties: his States-General. Philip convened the representatives from Burgundy in Dijon and those from the Netherlands in Brussels. His States-General met more frequently than the French. The duke wanted to arrange financial matters jointly with all his provinces, apportioning burdens on the basis of general consultations. The States-General in the kingdom of the Netherlands developed into the people's representative body.

Philip's son Charles (reigned 1433–1477) was impulsive and prepared to take greater risks than his father, as his nickname, the Bold, indicates. The decade that he ruled was a mixture of great success and terrible disasters.

The Spider

From 1461 to 1483 France was ruled by the inscrutable Louis XI, who had much in common with his great predecessor, Philip Augustus. He, too, was not a fighter. He, too, was shrewd, miserly, and ruthless. In Louis XI, though, these characteristics were more pronounced. His contemporaries referred to this brooding, dark-clad king as "the Spider."

The Spider was a bourgeois at heart. He hated aristocrats and their values. He was not interested in honor, but in power and money. He rarely used direct violence, finding intrigue and bribery sufficient to attain his goals. He was advised by astrologers before making any major decisions. Philip the Good could withstand his scheming opponent. Charles the Bold could not. He believed in an open, chivalrous way of fighting.

When he ascended the throne, Charles the Bold was in a strong position. Louis XI had generated considerable resentment among the people, and Philip the Good craftily fanned the flames of insurrection. To assist him, Charles the Bold crossed the border with his troops. A "League of General Welfare" was formed to fight the king, but Louis was not hated as much as the people in Dijon wanted to believe. Although Charles managed to take Louis XI prisoner, the invasion soon came to a standstill. Louis was released after he had made a series of important concessions, including the cession of his feudal rights to Flanders.

Charles withdrew to his own country. Louis continued to conspire against the Burgundians. He incited neighboring states against Charles and encouraged resentment

Cup made of jasper with cover mounted in gold, from fifteenth-century Burgundy

among his subjects over their taxes. The duke assessed them with far less tact than his father had done.

Charles's policy was much more aggressive than that of Philip the Good. He waged more wars, and waging war is expensive. Charles's subjects had little comprehension of their lord's expansive plans. They felt a kinship with their county and enjoyed their privileges. At first the Burgundian duke prospered. He managed to subjugate Gelre and conquer the region between his possessions in the Netherlands and Burgundy. Finally, he managed to persuade Frederick II

to offer him a royal crown.

Frederick's consent was the result of a marriage between Charles's only child, Mary, and the emperor's son Maximilian I in 1477. The royal crown would return to the family and bring a whole empire with it. The ceremonies were to be held in Trier, a Roman city in the Rhineland. The emperor and the duke entered the old bishop's town with pomp and circumstance. Messengers from Louis XI entered the gates in a less conspicuous manner. Gaining access to the emperor, they convinced him that his future son-in-law was unreliable. The night before

the coronation, the emperor left Trier in secret. Charles was furious, but Maximilian and Mary had met in Trier and would not forget each other.

Charles concentrated more than ever on his own expansionist policies. In 1476 he marched into the Jura Mountains with an enormous army. The Swiss had been bold enough to declare their freedom. The duke intended to crush them violently and quickly. The expedition became a catastrophe. Charles's knights, armed to the teeth, were beaten by the Swiss peasants. The Burgundians suffered severe defeats at

Miniature from the fourteenth century illustrating a scene from the book *Lancelot du Lac*, a romance about courtly love that was very popular in the Middle Ages

Granson and Murten. The Swiss even managed to seize the whole baggage train. This was quite a haul, since Charles always took jewels and expensive tapestries with him wherever he went to decorate his tent. The

Colored pen drawing from the *Great Chronicle of Burgundy* by Diebold Schilling depicting the battle at Murten (1476) that meant defeat for the Burgundians led by Charles the Bold

Swiss took this *Burgunderbeute* (Burgundy treasure) joyfully to Berne where it is still occasionally exhibited. Charles the Bold had taken enough works of art with him to fill many galleries.

There were more troubles ahead for Charles in 1477. The city of Nancy in Lorraine rebelled. The duke attacked it like a madman, but the weather was icy cold and the inhabitants defended themselves ferociously. The siege at Nancy was a notable failure. The troops fled in panic; the duke

disappeared. His body was found a few days later, frozen in the mud and half devoured by wolves.

Louis XI acted at once. Entering Burgundy, he occupied the whole duchy with no resistance from the people, who were tired of Charles's reckless reign. His daughter Mary inherited a divided empire full of unhappy subjects. The Netherlands took advantage of the situation. The States-General recognized her only on certain conditions, to which Mary submitted. She made great concessions to her subjects, confirming all their former rights and privileges. They also demanded that they never be taxed without the approval of the States-General or the proper authorities.

From the mixed assortment of duchies that Mary inherited, a Dutch nation might have developed, but Maximilian of Austria once again asked for her hand in marriage. Mary agreed immediately. As a result, her possessions became part of the Hapsburg patrimony. The marriage to Maximilian was a great success, both politically and personally, and they enjoyed a few happy years. Then, in 1482, Mary fell off her horse in what proved to be a fatal accident. The couple had a son, Philip the Fair, whose wife Joanna inherited the Spanish kingdom formed from Aragon and Castile. Their son was the great Hapsburg ruler, Charles V.

In the fourteenth and fifteenth centuries there were new concepts of government. With the growth of large unified states, more power fell into the hands of the bourgeois class. Society was no longer based on agriculture, but on urban industry and international trade. The dukes of Burgundy and the French court during these centuries encouraged artistic development, as did the papal court in Avignon and the cities of Florence and Siena in the fourteenth century. Ideas developed naturally out of the late medieval experiences of communal governments and the loss of faith in royalty and the papacy that resulted from the Hundred Years' War, papal schism, and the failure of the Crusades.

There was also a renewed interest in classical learning and culture, spurred by the reintroduction of texts through Arabic Spain to European universities in the thirteenth century, as well as Italy's interest in its rich heritage. It was in northern Italian cities that the Renaissance began, and a humanistic trend among scholars engaged in questioning the Church was first found in the north. Reformation, then, was to accompany the Renaissance.

TIME LINE

EUROPE POLITICAL HISTORY	EUROPE CULTURAL HISTORY	EVENTS IN THE REST OF THE WORLD

850 — **c.850** Establishment of a naval base in Pisa to ward off Muslim raids

900 —
910 — **911** Charles the Simple and Normandy buy the aid of the Norsemen
920 —
930 —
940 —
950 — **c.950** West Frankish Empire in chaos because of competing fiefdoms
955 Otto I, ruler of the German Empire, defeats the Magyars at Lechfield

c.950 Rise of medieval society by elimination of external threats and agricultural innovations; merchants settle at crossroads and rest stops

960 —
970 — **969** Conquest of Egypt by the Fatimids
980 —
987 Hugh Capet becomes king of the West Frankish Empire
990 —
1000 — **c.1000** Scandinavia becomes part of Western/Latin civilization
1005 Pisa repels the Muslims from Sardinia

c.1000 Rise of agricultural market production and greater specialization

1010 —
1013 King Swein of Denmark defeats English king Ethelred the Unready
1016 Canute the Great unites England, Denmark, and Norway

1014 Basil II of Byzantium defeats the Bulgarians
1031 Alfonso VII of Castile resumes his Christian offensive against the Muslims

1020 —
1030 —
1040 — **1042** Edward the Confessor takes the English throne

c.1040 Rabbi Shlomo Itschaki, known as Rashi, is born in Troyes
c.1050 Population growth is accompanied by increasing prosperity and deforestation; guilds evolve into interest groups for each trade
c.1075 Serfs employed as civil servants at the imperial court
1086 *Domesday Book*
1096 Persecution of Jews roused by the idea of crusades; origin of the Hasidic movement
c.1100 In Pisa, wealthy citizens organize in *communitas* (governing bodies); city charter written; Pisa has twelve to fifteen thousand inhabitants; *Memor-books* record Jewish martyrs

1050 — **c.1050** Diminishing anarchy in the French Empire; rise of the states of Sweden, Denmark, and Norway; rise of Poland as a Slavic empire
1060 —
1066 Battle of Hastings; William the Conqueror seizes England, divides the land among his followers, and introduces the feudal system
1070 —
1080 —
1090 — **1087** Death of William the Conqueror; feud among his sons
1100 —
1122 Concordat of Worms regulates the investiture of bishops
1125 Beginning of dynastic disputes between the Guelphs and Hohenstaufens

1110 —
1120 —
1125 Yuchs conquer northern China and found the Chin Empire
1127–1279 Yung dynasty in southern China

1130 — **1130–1150** Serious weakening of English royal position
1132 The commune of Pisa is recognized officially by the bishop
1137 Louis VII takes the French throne; marries Eleanor of Aquitaine
1140 —
1144 Uprising by the people of Rome; the pope leaves the city
1146 The Roman Senate elects a popular leader as emperor
1150 — **c.1150** Ideology of *Dominium Mundi*: the pope as ruler of the world

1145 Arnold of Brescia declared a heretic in Rome

Prehistory	Antiquity	Middle Ages	Renaissance	Modern History	Contemporary History

EUROPE POLITICAL HISTORY	EUROPE CULTURAL HISTORY	EVENTS IN THE REST OF THE WORLD

1150

1152 Marriage of Louis and Eleanor annulled; Frederick I Barbarossa becomes German emperor; Eleanor marries Henry Plantagenet

1153 Alliance of Pope Hadrian IV and German emperor Frederick Barbarossa

1154 Henry Plantagenet becomes king of English crown; reorganization of the English administrative system

1155

1157 Besançon parliament; Frederick I declares his divine right to power

1158 Roncaglia parliament; Frederick I demands absolute authority

1159 Cardinal Roland becomes Pope Alexander III; German emperor Frederick I appoints an antipope

1160

1161 Foundation of the Hanseatic League in Germany

1165 Pisa appoints a salaried chancellor; begin use of the cylinder seal

1170 Creation of the Lombardian League

1172 Invasion of Italy by Frederick I Barbarossa

1175

1176 Battle of Legnano, army of the German emperor defeated

1177 Frederick I concludes a peace treaty with Alexander III and the Lombardian League

1178–1180 Frederick I declares Henry the Lion's fiefs forfeit

1180–1214 King Philip Augustus II expands his power in much of the French Empire

1180

1184 Marriage of Frederick's son Henry VI and Constance of Sicily

1185

1189 Richard the Lionhearted succeeds Henry in England

1190 Frederick I Barbarossa dies in the Third Crusade, succeeded by Henry VI

1192–1333 Kamakura shogunate in Japan

1195

1197 Henry VI dies; his son, Frederick II, ascends the throne; dynastic feud

1198 Otto of Brunswick crowned emperor, supported by Pope Innocent III, who becomes guardian of the young Frederick II

1199 John Lackland becomes king of England

c.1200 Germanic tribes drive the Slavs back to the Vistula River (Germany); John Lackland forced back to Gascony (France); England and Norway establish close ties

1202–1204 Fourth Crusade; capture and plunder of Constantinople

1200

1203–1204 Innocent III promotes the Second Greater Bulgarian Empire to kingdom

1206 Ghingiz (Genghis) Khan founds the Mongol Empire

1205

1210

1211–1215 Mongol armies destroy the Chin Empire

1212–1250 Frederick II becomes German emperor

1214 Battle at Bouvines; Philip Augustus II strengthens his grip on France

1215 The Magna Carta exacted by vassals in England

1216 John Lackland and Innocent III die; end of the civil war in England

1217–1280 Haakon IV and Magnus the Lawmaker restore the Norwegian kingdom

1216 Fourth Lateran Council determines that Jews must wear the Star of David

1220

Prehistory	Antiquity	Middle Ages	Renaissance	Modern History	Contemporary History

EUROPE POLITICAL HISTORY	EUROPE CULTURAL HISTORY	EVENTS IN THE REST OF THE WORLD

1226 The Teutonic Order focuses on the areas east of the Oder
1227 Gregory IV forces Frederick II to go on a crusade
1229 German emperor Frederick II is crowned in Jerusalem, goes to battle against Pope Gregory IV and the Lombardian League; Louis IX the Saint brings order and justice to France

1227 Death of Ghingiz (Genghis) Khan, division of the empire among his sons

1235 First Bulgarian patriarchate

1241 Battle at Liegnitz ends Mongol offensive

1248–1254 Crusade led by Louis IX is stranded in Egypt

1250 Death of Frederick II; interregnum of the German Empire; Foljungar dynasty stimulates Swedish economy
c.1250 Relations among Italian oligarchies deteriorate; rise of the podesta; Reconquista of Spain halted; territorial principalities rise in peripheral areas of the German Empire
1254 Manfred succeeds Conrad IV king of Naples and Sicily in Italy

c.1250 Commercial aspect of the annual market fades after introduction of the bill of exchange; boom in long-term leases

1251 Reign of the Golden Horde

1256 Invasion of the Mongols in Persia
1258 Destruction of Baghdad by Mongol armies
1260 Mamlukes defeat the Mongols at Ain-Jalut

1258 Henry III on the English throne, forced to introduce government reforms

1261–1262 Old treaty ties Iceland and Greenland to the Norwegian king, Haakon the Old
1263–1265 Pope crowns Charles of Anjou king of Normandy

1266 Death of Manfred; Norsemen forced to relinquish the Isle of Man and the Hebrides

1270 Louis IX dies during crusade in Tunis

1272 Rudolf of Hapsburg becomes emperor of Germany, ending the interregnum
1272–1307 Expansion by Edward I of England toward Ireland, Wales, and Scotland

c.1275 Construction of large churches in Sweden

1274–1281 Attacks of the Mongols on Japan

1278 Emperor Rudolf of Germany declares Ottokar's fiefs forfeit

1279 Conquest of the Sung dynasty by Kubilai, founder of the Yuan dynasty

1282 Sicilian Vespers; Charles of Anjou banished; Peter of Aragon receives the crown of Sicily; power of Danish king diminished after creation of Danehof
1285–1314 Philip the Fair of France strengthens the government

1291 Acco, last Christian stronghold in the Near East, is lost; Swiss *Eidgenossenschaft* (eternal union) established among Uri, Schwyz, and Unterwalden; Rudolf of Hapsburg dies, succeeded by Adolf of Nassau
1294–1303 Reign of Pope Boniface VIII
1295 Empire divided by colonization of Poland

Prehistory	Antiquity	Middle Ages	Renaissance	Modern History	Contemporary History

	EUROPE POLITICAL HISTORY	EUROPE CULTURAL HISTORY	EVENTS IN THE REST OF THE WORLD
1300	**c.1300** Boniface forbids Philip to tax the French clergy **1300–1350** Italian cities evolve into city-states, dominated by an elite **1302** Papal bull *Unam Sanctum* **1303** Pope Boniface held prisoner by the French in Agnani **1304** Battle of the Spurs, French nobility defeated by Flemish citizens	**c.1300** Decline in population growth; property of French Jews is confiscated; Lübeck controls trade in the Baltic Sea	**1301** Osman I founds the Osman Empire
1305	**1305–1314** Clement V, archbishop of Bordeaux, becomes pope **1306–1333** King Vladislav IV of Poland is forced to relinquish extensive territory **1307** Start of the residence of the Holy See in Avignon, "Babylonian exile"; Church bureaucracy grows to hitherto unknown proportions	**1304–1374** Petrarch uses the term *Babylonian exile* to refer to the papal residence in Avignon, France **1307–1377** Loss of Church prestige due to corruption and simony (sale of church office)	**1307** First Catholic archbishopric in Beijing (Peking)
1310		**1310** Order of the Knights Templar is abolished by Pope Clement V	
1315		**1314** Leaders of the order executed in Paris by Philip IV the Fair	
1320			
1325			
1330	**1328** Philip VI of Valois takes the French crown, challenged by Edward III of England	**c.1330** Popular uprising in Ghent under Jacob de Artevelde; "Work and Freedom"	
1335	**1333–1370** Casimir the Great becomes king of Poland	**1333–1370** Jewish, Greek, and Armenian merchants protected in Polish cities	
1340	**1337** Hundred Years' War begins; Philip VI declares Edward III's fiefs forfeit **1340** Edward III lands on the Flemish coast		**c.1340** Hindu Empire in India evolves into center of resistance against Islam
1345			
1350	**1346** Battle of Crécy; the French are defeated **1347** English king Edward III conquers Calais	**1346** At Crécy, the English use archers	**1346** Urosh IV becomes emperor of the Serbs and Greeks
1355	**1350** Death of Philip VI; succeeded by John the Good **c.1350** German emperors try to retain control in Italy **1354** Bernabo Visconti seizes power in Milan	**c.1350** Black Death claims a third of the European population; spiritualism on the rise; plague epidemic causes renewed persecution of Jews; agricultural production specialized into monoculture, e.g. grain from the Baltics and wool from England; rise of new urban centers	
1360	**1356** The Black Prince defeats the French at Poitiers, takes John the Good prisoner; Golden Bull, college of elective monarchs, elects the German emperor **1357** French crown prince Charles V announces government reforms **1358** Etienne Marcel takes over the government of Paris; uprising of the *Jacquerie* (French peasants); Charles the Bad of Navarre restores order as regent	**c.1360** France ravaged by plundering groups of mercenaries	**c.1360** Tamerlane, innovator of the Mongol world empire
1365	**1363** Philip the Bold obtains duchy of Burgundy as *apanage* from Charles V the Wise **1364** Charles V the Wise returns to a monarchist Paris		
1370	**1366** Peace of Bretigny **1367** Charles V the Wise resumes the war **1370** Peace of Stalsund; cities of the Hanseatic League are made toll-exempt	**1367** French army, led by Bertrand de Guesclin, utilizes guerrilla tactics	

Prehistory	Antiquity	Middle Ages	Renaissance	Modern History	Contemporary History

	EUROPE POLITICAL HISTORY	EUROPE CULTURAL HISTORY	EVENTS IN THE REST OF THE WORLD
1375	**1375** English hold only the citadels of Calais, Bordeaux, and Bayonne **1375–1380** Margaretha becomes regent of Norway and Denmark **1376** Death of the Black Prince; young Richard succeeds Edward III; Swabian league of cities formed **1377** Pope Gregory IX moves back to Rome **1378** Gregory dies; Urban VI becomes pope in Rome; antipope Clement VII settles in Avignon; the Great Schism divides the Christian Church	**1378** Schism causes cry for Church reforms	
1380	**1380** Death of Charles V; Crown Prince Charles VI is still a minor; Louis of Anjou rules the French Empire **1381** Unrest among the English people, led by Watt Tyler		**1380** First Russian victory over the Tartars
1385	**1384** Annexation of Flanders, Nevers, and Franche-Comté to Burgundy		
1390	**1389** Margaretha made queen of Sweden		
1395			
1400	**1397** Union of Kalmar **1399** King Richard of England taken prisoner by Henry IV of Lancaster **c.1400** Foundation of central institutions in German principalities; continuous civil war between Italian city-states	**c.1400** Italian cities hire army commanders (*condottieri*) whom they pay for their services	
1405	**1404** Death of Philip the Bold of Burgundy		
1410	**1407** John the Fearless, duke of Burgundy, kills Louis of Orléans, beginning the battle between Armagnacs and Bourguignons **1409** Council of Pisa; both popes are deposed; election of Pope John XXII causes the coexistence of three popes; Florence subjects Pisa **1410** Battle of Tannenberg; Teutonic Order defeated by Poland **1412** Birth of Joan of Arc		
1415	**1415** Council of Constance; conciliar theory formulated; Henry IV lands on the Normandy coast; Battle of Agincourt **1417** Martin V moves to Rome; distances himself from the conciliar movement		
1420	**1419** John the Fearless is assassinated, succeeded by Philip the Good **1420** Treaty of Troyes **1422** Death of Henry V and Charles VI; Charles VII rules France	**1419–1467** Wealth and culture flower in Burgundy, setting the tone for all of Europe **1422** During Charles VII's reign a pessimist mood settles over the French people, impoverished and disillusioned by the war with England	
1425	**1425–1430** Holland, Zeeland, Hainault, Brabant, and Limburg added to Burgundy		

Prehistory	Antiquity	Middle Ages	Renaissance	Modern History	Contemporary History

	EUROPE POLITICAL HISTORY	EUROPE CULTURAL HISTORY	EVENTS IN THE REST OF THE WORLD
1425			
	1427 The English besiege Orléans, part of the One Hundred Years' War		
	1429 Joan of Arc ends the siege of Orléans; Charles VII crowned king		
1430	**1430–1431** Joan of Arc taken prisoner by the English and burned at the stake as a heretic in Rouen		
	1431–1449 Councils of Basel, Ferrara, and Florence (Italy)	**1431** Joan of Arc becomes symbol of French resistance against English rule	
1435	**1435** Treaty of Arras, reconciliation between Charles VII of France and Philip the Good of Burgundy; Peace of Vordingborg; Danish king again defeated by the Hanseatic League		
	1436 French army enters Paris		
	1439 Decision to reunify with the Eastern Church; antipope Felix V; start of a new schism		
1440	**1440** Frederick III elected Hapsburg emperor		
	1442 Kingdoms of Naples and Sicily become part of the united kingdom of Aragon		
	1447 In Milan, Francesco Sforza assumes power from the Viscontis		
1450	**1449–1450** Rouen and Cherbourg capitulate to the French	**c.1450** Renaissance	
	1453 Only Calais remains in English hands; end of the Hundred Years' War		**1453** Constantinople seized by the Ottoman army
1460	**1461–1483** Louis XI the Spider ascends the French throne		**1462** Ivan III the Great proclaims himself czar of all of Russia
	1466 Fall of Marienburg; Teutonic Order becomes subject to the Polish-Lithuanian Empire		
	1467 Charles the Bold inherits a divided empire of Burgundy and the Netherlands		
	1468 Norway forced to relinquish the Orkneys and Shetland Islands		
1470	**1474** Invasion of France by Charles the Bold; takes the French king Louis XI prisoner		
	1476 The army of Charles the Bold suffers serious defeat against the Swiss		
	1477 Death of Charles the Bold at the siege of Nancy; Maximilian of Austria marries Mary of Burgundy		
1480	**1482** Mary of Austria dies		
	1483–1498 Charles VIII of France lays claim to the kingdom of Naples		
1490	**1492** Last Moorish rulers driven from Spain	**1492** Columbus discovers America	
	1494 Pisa manages to get rid of Florentine dominion		
	1496 Marriage between Philip of Austria and Joanna, heiress to the Spanish throne		
1500	**c.1500** End of influence of Germany and the Hanseatic League on northern and eastern Europe		
1510			
1520			
1530			
	1532 Sweden secedes from the Union of Kalmar		
1540			
1550			
	1558 Siena annexed to the city-state of Florence		
1560			

Prehistory	Antiquity	Middle Ages	Renaissance	Modern History	Contemporary History

Glossary

Alexander III pope (1159–1181); opponent of Frederick Barbarossa who recognized him in 1177.

apanage region in the French Empire controlled by the younger brothers of the French king. Burgundy was an apanage until the Hundred Years' War.

Armagnacs supporters of Louis of Orléans who joined Bernard of Armagnac after the former's death and who started a bloody civil war with the Bourguignons.

Arnold of Brescia (d. 1155) popular preacher who criticized the Church's political power; his sermons caused a rebellion in Rome in 1146, after which the Senate regained its power; the pope was aided by Frederick Barbarossa in assassinating Arnold.

Babylonian exile (1305–1376) period when the popes resided in Avignon because Italy was divided by feuds among noblemen; Avignon became a bureaucratic center of corrupt popes and prelates.

Battle of the Spurs (July 11, 1302) when an untrained Flemish infantry army of civilians defeated armed French knights.

Becket, Thomas archbishop of Canterbury (1162–1170); opponent of Henry II Plantagenet, who took away the authority of the ecclesiastical courts; killed in 1170, after which the Church and the English people turned against Henry.

bills of exchange IOU's substituting for money, enabling merchants to travel without fear of theft.

Boniface VIII pope (1294–1303); when he forbade Philip IV the Fair of France to tax the Church, the latter had him imprisoned in 1303 with the people's support.

Bourguignons supporters of the Burgundian dukes John the Fearless and Philip the Good; they fought a civil war against the Armagnacs and obtained the support of the English king who occupied France between 1415 and 1436.

civil rights privilege of the city charter whereby fleeing serfs, who had lived in a place of refuge for one year and one day, became free citizens; usually the liege lords of a city stipulated that their own serfs were excluded.

Calais port on the west coast of France, which was conquered by Edward III following the battle of Crécy in 1347 and which continued as an English bridgehead until the sixteenth century.

Canute the Great king of England (1016–1035); united England, Norway, and Denmark into one kingdom; Church recognized him as a Christian king; after his death the kingdom fell apart and Edward the Confessor became king.

Carthusians monastic order which stressed penance, solitude, and asceticism; founded at the end of the eleventh century.

Catherine of Siena fourteenth-century Dominican nun who persuaded the pope in 1376 to move back to Rome and led the popular movement against the antipapal Italian cities.

Charles V the Wise king of France (1364–1380); concluded the Peace of Bretigny in 1360 when he was still crown prince; restored and reorganized France and resumed the war.

Charles VI king of France (1380–1422); concluded a truce with England in 1396; because of his madness, his relatives were fighting for power, especially his brother Louis of Orléans and his uncle Philip the Bold.

Charles VII king of France (1422–1461); thanks to Joan of Arc he was crowned king in 1429; concluded the Peace of Arras and caused the complete expulsion of the English from France (except for Calais) in 1453.

Charles of Anjou king of Naples (1266–1285); with the pope's support he expelled the Ghibelline rulers from the Norman kingdom of Sicily; in 1282 he lost Sicily and moved to Naples.

Charles the Bold duke of Burgundy (1467–1477); expanded the Burgundian Empire; in 1476 he was defeated by the Swiss; in 1477 he died during the siege of Nancy, and Louis XI of France occupied Burgundy.

Children's Crusade (1212) expedition of armies of children from France and Germany to Palestine; the French largely fell into the hands of Islamic slave traders; the pope ordered the German army to return; many children died from exhaustion.

Cistercians monastic order founded in 1098 in France near Citeaux; their emphasis was on austerity and simplicity.

city charter privileges granted by a liege lord to free cities in exchange for political support; privileges consisted of the administration of justice, toll exemption, city walls, and civil rights.

colonization thirteenth-century claiming of hitherto uncultivated areas in Europe.

commune board of free cities that ruled independently of the liege lords; city aldermen, mostly rich merchants who had absolute power, were assisted by an advisory board of senators called consuls.

condottieri mercenary generals who conducted war by order of Italian cities; supported by the population; ruled the cities with military authority.

Council of Basel (1431–1449) council of the opponents of Pope Eugenius IV, who tried to abolish the council's authority and received an increasing amount of support among Christians who wanted a united Church; in 1437 the council appointed an antipope who abdicated in 1449, thus ending its authority.

Council of Constance (1414–1418) council that ended the Schism that had forced a number of popes to abdicate; it constituted the Church's highest authority.

Council of Pisa (1409) Church's highest authority at this time; council of prelates that deposed the popes in Rome and Avignon and appointed a new one.

Crécy town on the west coast of France where the French army, consisting of knights, was destroyed in 1346 by the English infantry and opened the way for Edward III to conquer Calais.

curia regis Anglo-Saxon board that advised the king, established by William the Conqueror; department of finance was called the exchequer after the cloth on which the monies were counted.

Domesday Book land registry introduced during the reign of William the Conqueror in which all property of the inhabitants of England was registered for tax purposes.

dominium mundi papal domination of the world; during the thirteenth century, dominium mundi reached the acme of its power, especially in the person of Innocent III.

Edward III king of England (1327–1377); proclaimed himself king of France in 1337, thus unleashing the Hundred Years' War; reshaped the army into lance fighters and archers instead of heavily armed horsemen.

Edward, the Black Prince (1330–1376) son of Edward III and an important commander during the Hundred Years' War; destroyed regions of southern France and took John the Good prisoner at Poitiers.

Eighth Crusade (1270) expedition led by Saint Louis IX to Tunis; Moors threatened Naples' trade position in the Mediterranean; during the siege of Tunis an epidemic broke out and Louis died.

Eleanor of Aquitaine heiress to the kingdom of Aquitaine and wife of Louis VII of France who had the marriage annulled in 1152; as revenge she married Henry II Plantagenet of England, giving him the western part of the French Empire.

Ethelred the Unready king of England (979–1016); introduced danegeld as a direct tax to buy off the Norsemen; when he discontinued this practice, he was expelled by the Norsemen who founded an empire in England under Canute.

Fairs annual commercial fairs at central rural locations in Europe in the thirteenth century.

Flagellants groups of people who publicly flogged themselves as a way of doing penance, popular during the plague; banned by the Church when the movement demanded reforms.

Fifth Crusade (1217–1221) expedition during which Lisbon was conquered in 1217 and Damietta in Egypt in 1218; against the pope's wishes the crusaders tried to conquer Egyptian territory in exchange for Jerusalem, but this attempt failed.

Flanders duchy of the French king, beginning in the twelfth century, which was economically dependent on England for its textile manufacture; when Edward III prohibited the export of wool in 1337, Flanders rebelled against France; the uprising was crushed in 1340.

Fourth Crusade (1202–1204) expedition by French knights; they took Byzantium with the aid of Venice and founded a western-style empire.

Frederick I Barbarossa Holy Roman Emperor of the German Empire (1152–1190); as a scion of the Hohenstaufen family he made peace with the Guelph leader, Henry of Saxony; strengthened his power and withdrew many privileges from the princes and dukes of his realm; fought against the rebellious Lombard League, the Guelphs, rebellious noblemen, and the pope; died during the Third Crusade.

Frederick II emperor of the Holy Roman Empire of Germany (1212–1250); was supported by Innocent III, but left the German noblemen to their own devices and harshly ruled the empire of Sicily; in 1228 he was crowned king of Jerusalem.

free city settlement populated by craftsmen and artisans who lived outside the feudal structure and had their own government and legal system; the liege lord granted these free areas privileges, such as toll exemption, the right to build walls, and citizenship for the inhabitants.

German Hansa alliance of North German and Dutch merchants and commercial towns founded in approximately 1150; had a monopoly on trade in the Baltic Sea and the North Sea; grew into a powerful alliance of cities, continuing into the fifteenth century.

Ghibellines supporters of the House of Hohenstaufen and proponents of the rule of a strong emperor over the Church; fought the Guelphs; in 1268 they were defeated for good.

Greenland island off the North American coast, discovered in 982 by the Viking Eric the Red; was colonized and had trade contacts with Norway and Iceland; politically tied to Norway in c. 1260.

Gregory IX pope (1227–1241); excommunicated Frederick II because of his unwillingness to go on a crusade; supported the Lombard League against Frederick's expansion of power.

Guelphs supporters of the House of Guelph and proponents of a monarchy with little influence, powerful vassals, and an autonomous Church; from 1125 they fought the Ghibellines and defeated the last scion of the Hohenstaufen family.

du Guesclin, Bertrand (1318–1380) nobleman from Gascony whom Charles V the Wise appointed supreme commander of the army; he trained unemployed mercenaries and fought a guerilla war against Edward the Black.

guilds organizations of merchants and artisans who supervised the quality and price of manufacture and the working conditions; only guild members were allowed to exercise their craft in the cities.

Hansa international league of merchants that arose from companies of travelers organized for safety reasons; the hansas protected their trade interests by acquiring product monopolies and controlling prices; the hansas grew into alliances of commercial towns.

Hansa of the Seventeen Towns alliance of Flemish and northern French commercial towns that controlled trade between western and southern Europe in the thirteenth century; textile products from Flanders were its focal point.

Hasidism Jewish religious movement in the eleventh and twelfth centuries that strictly adhered to the laws of the Bible and Talmud; especially influential in the Rhineland.

Harold Godwinson king of England in 1066; the personal advisor to Edward the Confessor; in 1066 he became king and fought the other pretenders to the throne: Norse king Harold Hardrada and Norman William the Conqueror; defeated Harold but died in the Battle of Hastings while fighting William.

Hastings town on the English coast where William the Conqueror landed in 1066 and battled the army of King Harold; Normans defeated the Anglo-Saxons exhausted by the battle against the Norsemen; Harold died and William became king of England.

Henry the Lion of Saxony duke of Saxony and Bavaria (1154–1180); vassal of Frederick Barbarossa; a Guelph, but made peace with Frederick in 1152; when Frederick fought the Lombard League in 1177, Henry refused to help him because of his own ambitions; Frederick deprived him of his dukedom as punishment, and Henry ended his life in exile in England.

Henry V king of England (1414–1422); defeated the Armagnacs in 1415 and occupied large areas of France, which enabled John the Fearless, duke of Burgundy, to obtain power in Paris.

Henry II Plantagenet king of England (1154–1189); through his marriage to Eleanor of Aquitaine, he acquired the western portion of the French Empire.

Friars minor (Franciscans) monastic order founded by Francis of Assisi in 1223; mendicants were not allowed to own anything; monasteries were also supposed to share their possessions with the poor.

Hugh Capet king of France (987–996); before he rose to power the French Empire had been fragmented as a result of the power of the county rulers; Hugh and his descendants, the Capetians, gained strength and slowly reunited the empire; dynasty ruled France until 1328 when the last Capetian king, Charles IV, died without a male heir.

Hundred Years' War (1337–1453) war between France and England, which still possessed areas in France; immediate cause was a dispute about the succession to the French throne; by 1453, England had lost all in France except for Calais.

Iceland island in the North Sea discovered and colonized by the Vikings in the ninth century; had commercial ties with Norway and was politically tied to the Norse king around 1260.

Innocent III pope (1198–1216); restored papal authority in the papal states and established *dominium mundi* by playing foreign rulers against one another, granting political support.

interdict papal sanction whereby citizens of the territory of a sinner are excluded from all religious ceremonies; in this manner the pope could pit the populace against the perpetrator.

interregnum (1256–1273) period of the German Empire without an emperor, because after the death of the Holy Roman emperor the electors were unable to agree on a new candidate.

Jacquerie farmers rebellion in 1358 by "Les Jacques," peasants around Paris, against their lords in response to years of oppression and the battle lost at Poitiers, crushed by Charles the Bad.

Joan of Arc (1412–1431) peasant girl, driven by visions, who broke the siege of Orléans and had Charles VII crowned king in Reims; her attack on Paris failed; was extradited to the English in 1430, who burned her at the stake as a heretic; became the symbol of French resistance against England.

John II the Good king of France (1350–1364); was taken prisoner at the battle of Poitiers in 1356; after paying ransom he was released but voluntarily returned when a French hostage escaped.

John the Fearless duke of Burgundy (1404–1419); son of Philip the Bold; was probably responsible for having Louis of Orléans killed, whose supporters, the Armagnacs, then attacked John's followers, the Bourguignons; John entered an alliance with the English in 1415.

John Lackland king of England (1199–1216); slowly lost his French territories to Philip II Augustus; after his ally Otto IV had been defeated by Philip Augustus in 1214, he resigned himself to his loss.

kabbala Jewish secret mystic movement from the twelfth and thirteenth centuries which explained the Bible by way of numbers and mysticism.

kehilla Jewish community in the Middle Ages; the religious and administrative authority; Jews were autonomous and based their government on the Talmud.

knightly order brotherhood of Christian noblemen who fought Muslims and were founded in the West; examples are the Knights Hospitaler and the Knights Templars; secular orders such as the Order of the Garter were honorary.

Knights Hospitalers society of Christian knights who fought Muslims; order grew out of the eleventh-century pilgrims' hospital in the Holy Land; when noblemen of the brotherhood became their leaders, the order took on a military character.

Stephen Langton archbishop of Canterbury (1206–1228); mediator between John Lackland and rebellious vassals; added rights of the Church and the people to the Magna Carta.

Latin Empire western rule of Constantinople (1204–1261); founded after the Christian conquest during the Fourth Crusade; empire was forced to fight border wars and rebellions; in 1261 Michael Paleologus restored the Byzantine Empire.

Lombard League alliance of Italian cities that rebelled against Frederick I Barbarossa in 1167 after he revoked their royal privileges of coinage, tolls, and administration of justice, league defeated him in 1176.

Louis VII Capetian king of France (1137–1180); by annulling his marriage to Eleanor he lost a large portion of his empire to Henry II Plantagenet; successfully pitted the French barons against Henry.

Louis IX the Saint king of France (1226–1270); during his rule peace and calm reigned; provided just legislation and abolished trial by judgment; in this manner he increased the popularity of the monarchy and the kingdom's unity.

Louis XI the Spider king of France (1461–1483); his intrigues slowly eroded the power of Burgundy; he bought off Edward IV, English ally to Charles the Bold, in 1475; following the latter's death in 1477 he occupied Burgundy.

Louis of Orléans brother of Charles VI who assumed actual power of the French Empire between 1392 and 1407 due to Charles VI's madness; in 1407 he was assassinated, probably on the orders of his cousin John, duke of Burgundy.

Magna Carta manifest issued by John Lackland in 1215 under pressure from rebellious barons; rights and obligations of both king and barons were set forth in this document; taxation without approval by the barons was impossible.

Marcel, Etienne Parisian market superintendent who gained control of the administration of Paris in 1358; he wanted to limit royal authority and control the war finances; when the Jacquerie was suppressed, he was murdered.

Mary of Burgundy daughter of Charles the Bold; duchess of Burgundy (1477–1482); had to concede on many matters to the Netherlands States-General; married Maximilian II of Austria, and their kingdom became part of the Hapsburg Empire.

market superintendents authorities appointed by the local lord during annual fairs; they granted licenses to notaries and money changers, appointed order troops, and administered justice.

market peace legal status of the annual fairs, which were outside of local law; annual fairs were autonomous and had their own administration of justice and were controlled by the superintendents.

masterpiece proof of competence that an apprentice, a craftsman in training, had to complete to become a master and start his own business; in this manner the guilds were able to control the number of established businesses.

Matins of Bruges insurrection on May 18, 1302, by the Clauwaerts, the pro-English Flemish people against the French knights in Bruges, who had come to the assistance of the Francophile Flemish elite; many of the French aristocrats were killed during this insurrection.

ministeriales vassals and trusted followers of the German emperor who fulfilled high offices in the emperor's service and could thus become free; Frederick I Barbarossa expanded his power by appointing ministeriales.

money changers bankers who exchanged the various currencies during annual fairs; booked a small percentage of profit on the transactions; also dealt in bills of exchange and IOU's and extended money loans at exorbitant interest rates; these practices

were condemned by the Church.

Mongols Asiatic tribes who conquered the Russian principalities in the thirteenth century and threatened the German principalities; defeated the Polish armies and the knights of the Teutonic Order; thereafter they slowly withdrew southward.

Normandy duchy on the French west coast where the Norsemen had made their home in 911; Normans established the kingdom of Sicily in 1061; in 1066 William the Conqueror conquered England; in 1204 Normandy was incorporated into the French Empire.

Norsemen north Germanic tribes from Scandinavia who raided the coasts of Europe and undertook marauding expeditions; conquered England in 1013; between 1016 and 1035, Canute the Great, a Dane, was king of England; in 1066 the Norsemen were defeated by Harold.

Orléans city in the French duchy of Berry on the side of Charles VII and beleaguered by the English between 1427 and 1429; in 1429, the city was freed by a French army led by Joan of Arc.

Otto IV of Brunswick emperor of the German Empire (1198–1214); in 1214, Otto concluded an alliance with John Lackland, king of England, to jointly attack Philip Augustus of France, who supported the pretenders to the German throne; defeated at battle of Bouvines in 1214.

parlementum civitatis town parliament or meeting of the people in free cities, where citizens could express their complaints and lodge requests; parliament exercised no influence on the town council because a few wealthy families were in power.

Peace of Arras (1435) peace treaty between Charles VII and Philip the Good, under which Philip agreed to withdraw in exchange for the region of Burgundy; Charles was then able to concentrate on the English and slowly expel them from French lands.

Peace of Bretigny truce concluded in 1360 between Charles V the Wise of France and Edward III of England in which Edward agreed to renounce his claims to the French throne in exchange for one third of France. In 1367, Charles declared the peace invalid.

Peace of Stralsund (1370) agreement between the German Hanseatic League and Denmark in which the cities of the Hanseatic League were exempted from tolls; Danish tolls to enter the Baltic Sea were the cause of war.

Philip II Augustus king of France (1180–1223); annexed the French territories that had been apportioned to the English king in 1152; expanded his powers by instituting a nonfeudal government system and forged the French kingdom into a powerful unity.

Philip IV the Fair king of France (1285–1314); his wars against England and Flanders caused a financial crisis; he confiscated the property of the Knights Templar, the Lombardian bankers, and the Jews, whom he expelled from his kingdom; he ended the secular power of the pope.

Philip VI Valois king of France (1328–1350); seized the French territories of Edward III, after which the latter proclaimed himself king of France; Hundred Years' War erupted not long after.

Philip the Good duke of Burgundy (1419–1467); asked for English aid in his fight against the Armagnacs; finally acquired Burgundy and Flanders upon the Peace of Arras and annexed Holland, Brabant, Limburg, Namur, and Luxembourg.

plague disease of humans and rats spread by parasitic insects, usually fleas, biting humans when their rat hosts died; buboes (egg-sized swellings) formed in lymph nodes of victims; also spread by infection and contact; final septicemic phase caused dark purple skin color, which led to name Black Death; killed a third of Europe's population in the fourteenth century.

podestà dictator who ruled Italian cities as an absolute ruler representing the interests of the aristocracy; usually appointed at the request of cities that were divided by the disputes between aristocrats.

Poitiers city in central France where Edward the Black Prince of England destroyed the French army in 1356 with an English army of archers and lancers; John the Good, the French king, was taken prisoner.

Rashi eleventh-century Jewish rabbi; lived in Troyes, France; wrote commentaries on the Bible and the Talmud still in use today.

Richard I the Lion Heart king of England (1189–1199); participated in the Third Crusade and warred against Philip II Augustus, who undermined Richard's position by supporting his brother John Lackland.

Roman king designation of the emperor of the German or Holy Roman Empire before he was crowned emperor.

Roncaglia town in Italy and site of a diet or council in 1158 during which Frederick I Barbarossa demanded all royal privileges, such as levying of tolls, coinage, and jurisdiction, which resulted in rebellion by the nobility and the cities.

routiers mercenaries during the Hundred Years' War who were dismissed after the Peace of Bretigny and proceeded to raid the countryside; Bertrand du Guesclin assembled them and after 1370 they conducted a successful guerilla war against the English in southern France.

Rudolf of Hapsburg emperor of the German Empire (1273–1291); elected by the elective monarchs; increased his power by defeating the Bohemian king Ottokar and by annexing his territories in Austria, Carinthia, and Styria.

Salic Law rule in some noble families of Europe forbidding the succession of females or descendants through the female line to titles or offices.

Schism (1378–1417) division in the Church which occurred when the cardinals elected Clement VII as pope because they were dissatisfied with Urban VI; during this time there were two popes, one in Avignon and one in Rome; both were supported by competing secular rulers who expanded their influence in this manner.

Senate of Rome commune of Rome elected in 1144, after a popular uprising; after a power struggle with the popes, the Senate ultimately was given authority in local matters.

Seventh Crusade (1248–1254) expedition led by Louis IX the Saint to Damietta in Egypt where the Muslims took him prisoner; his alliance with the Mongols against the Muslims failed.

Sicilian Vespers rebellion in 1282 by the Sicilians against the French rule of Charles of Anjou; during this uprising, all Frenchmen in Palermo were killed; Sicily offered the crown to Peter of Aragon.

Sixth Crusade (1228) expedition led by Frederick II, during which he obtained Jerusalem by negotiating with the Muslims; he was crowned king of Jerusalem; in 1244 the Muslims reconquered Jerusalem.

steward administrator in France having a fixed salary who was directly supervised by the king; in this manner, an administrative apparatus loyal to the king was created, increasing his power.

Talmud Jewish document, continuously revised, encompassing all legal and religious discussions which were handed down orally by the Jewish people until they were written down in 500; constituted the basis for the government of Jewish communities in Europe.

Tannenberg (1430) a place in Poland where the battle between the Teutonic Order and the Polish and Lithuanian armies took place; German knights were defeated.

Teutonic Order order of knights who founded a powerful state in the thirteenth century in northern Germany and the Baltic States; knights were defeated in the battle of Tannenberg; by the end of the fifteenth century, they had lost their political influence.

Third Crusade (1189–1192) following the taking of Jerusalem in 1187, Frederick Barbarossa, Philip II Augustus, and Richard I the Lion Heart traveled to Palestine; Christians conquered the fortress of Acre, but Jerusalem remained in Turkish hands; mutual strife forced the Christians to return.

three-course rotation agricultural system introduced in the tenth century; land was cultivated two years and lay fallow the third, preventing exhaustion of soil.

trial by ordeal Germanic tradition whereby God would indicate the guilty party in legal disputes by way of trials and ritual duels; the Church considered this practice superstitious; Saint Louis attempted to abolish the custom.

Tyler, Wat (d. 1381) led a peasant uprising in 1381 in England which erupted after tax increases; Richard II acceded to Tyler's demands, but the mayor of London killed Tyler and the rebellion was crushed forcibly.

Union of Kalmar (1397) union of Norway, Denmark, and Sweden forged by Margaretha, regent of Denmark and Norway, and acknowledged by the Swedes in 1389, the kingdoms remained autonomous; in 1523, Sweden became independent.

van Artevelde, Jacob (d. 1340) aristocrat from Ghent, leader of the Flemish rebellion against France; tried in vain to create an alliance of towns under the English king who was recognized as the king of France; was murdered in 1340.

Venice lagoon in Italy which grew into Europe's first commercial settlement; in the tenth century, Venice became an independent political entity, which looked to Byzantium for trade and cultural interchange.

William the Conqueror king of England (1066–1087); a Norman duke who defeated King Harold at Hastings in 1066 and conquered England; established a centralized monarchy, granting estates to loyal followers but retaining power; it took a full century before the Norman occupiers merged with the Anglo-Saxons.

Bibliography

Growth and Prosperity

Duby, G. *The Early Growth of the European Economy.* London, 1974.

Lopez, R. J. *The Commercial Revolution of the Middle Ages, 950–1350.* New York, 1976.

Pounds, N. J. G. *An Economic History of Medieval Europe.* New York, 1975.

Towns and Cities

Hilton, R. H. *English and French Towns in Feudal Society.* Cambridge, 1992.

Little, L. K. *Religious Poverty and the Profit Economy of Medieval Europe.* Ithaca, 1983.

Mundy, J. H. *The Medieval Town.* Princeton, 1985.

Rivalry Along the Channel

Fawtier, R. *The Capetian Kings of France.* London, 1982.

Hallam, E. M. *Capetian France, 987–1328.* London, 1980.

Hallam, H. E. *Rural England, 1066–1348.* London, 1981.

Stafford, P. *Unification and Conquest: A Political and Social History of England in the Tenth and Eleventh Centuries.* London, 1989.

Popes and Emperors

Bartlett, R. *The Making of Europe: Conquest, Colonization and Cultural Change, 950–1350.* London, 1993.

Gillingham, J. B. *The Kingdom of Germany in the High Middle Ages.* London, 1971.

Hyde, J. K. *Society and Politics in Medieval Italy.* London, 1983.

Munz, P. *Frederick Barbarossa: A Study in Medieval Politics.* London, 1983.

Rulers in Europe

Abulafia, D. *Frederick II: A Medieval Emperor.* London, 1988.

Davies, R. R. *The British Isles, 1100–1500: Comparisons, Contrasts and Connections.* Edinburgh, 1988.

Haverkamp, A. *Medieval Germany, 1056–1273.* Oxford, 1988.

Hyde, J. K. *Society and Politics in Medieval Italy.* London, 1983.

Runciman, S. *The Sicilian Vespers: The History of the Mediterranean World in the Later Thirteenth Century.* Cambridge, 1982.

Strayer, J. R. *The Reign of Philip the Fair.* Princeton, 1980.

Warren, W. L. *The Governance of Norman and Angevin England, 1086–1272.* London, 1987.

The Late Middle Ages

Dykema, A. and Oberman, H. A., eds. *Anticlericalism in Late Medieval and Early Modern Europe.* Leiden, 1991.

Given-Wilson, C., and Curteis A. *The Black Death: Natural and Human Disasters in Medieval Europe.* London, 1984.

Gottfried, R. S. *The Black Death.* London, 1983.

Hale, J. R. *Renaissance Europe.* London, 1985.

Miskimin, H. A. *The Economy of Early Renaissance Europe.* Englewood Cliffs, 1969.

Schildhauer, J. *The Hansa: History and Culture.* Leipzig, 1985.

Jewish Culture in the Middle Ages

Ashtor, E. *The Jews and the Mediterranean Economy, 10th–15th Centuries.* London 1983.

Cohen, J. *The Friars and the Jews: The Evolution of Medieval Anti-Judaism.* Ithaca, 1983.

Cohen, M. R. *Under Crescent and Cross: The Jews in the Middle Ages.* Princeton, 1994.

Katz, J. *Tradition and Crisis: Jewish Society at the End of the Middle Ages.* London, 1985.

Stow, K. R. *Alienated Minority: The Jews of Medieval Latin Europe.* Cambridge, 1992.

The Hundred Years' War

Brown, A. L. *The Governance of Late Medieval England 1272–1461.* London, 1989.

Davies, R. R. *The British Isles, 1100–1500: Comparisons, Contrasts and Connections.* Edinburgh, 1988.

Fowler, K. *The Age of Plantagenet and Valois.* London, 1980.

Lander, J. R. *The Limitations of English Monarchy in the Later Middle Ages.* Toronto, 1988.

Ormrod, W. M. T*he Reign of Edward III: Crown and Political Society in England, 1327–1377.* London, 1993.

Warner, M. *Joan of Arc: The Image of Female Heroism.* London, 1983.

Emperors, Princes, and Dukes

Du Boulay, F. R. H. *Germany in the Later Middle Ages.* London, 1983.

Jones, P. J. *The Malatesa of Rimini and the Papal State.* London, 1974.

Martines, L., ed. *Violence and Civil Disorder in Italian Cities, 1200–1500.* Los Angeles, 1973.

Waley, D. *The Italian City-republics.* London, 1969.

Central Europe During the Middle Ages

Christiansen, E. *The Northern Crusades: The Baltic and the Catholic Frontier, 1100–1525.* London, 1980.

Fennell, J. *The Crisis of Medieval Russia, 1200–1304.* London, 1983.

Halperin, C. J. *The Mongol Impact on Russian History.* London, 1987.

Schildhauer, J. *The Hansa: History and Culture.* Leipzig, 1985.

Burgundy

Vaughan, R. *Valois Burgundy.* London, 1975

———. *Philip the Good: The Apogee of Burgundy.* London/New York, 1970.

Further Reading

Biel, Timothy L. *The Age of Feudalism.* San Diego, 1994.

Brooks, Polly S. *Queen Eleanor: Independent Spirit of the Medieval World.* New York, 1983.

————. *Beyond the Myth: The Story of Joan of Arc.* New York, 1990.

Cairns, Trevor. *Medieval Knights.* New York, 1992.

Corbishley, Mike. *Middle Ages.* New York, 1990.

Dana, Barbara. *Young Joan.* New York, 1991.

Hernandez, Xavier, and Ballonga, Jordi. *Lebek: A City of Northern Europe through the Ages.* Boston, 1991.

History of Britain Series. *The Saxons and the Normans.* Auburn, ME, 1990.

————. *The Middle Ages.* Auburn, ME, 1990.

Jones, Madeline. *Knights and Castles.* North Pomfret, VT, 1991.

Konigsburg, E. L. *A Proud Taste for Scarlet and Miniver.* (F) New York, 1973.

Lace, William W. *The Battle of Hastings.* San Diego, 1996.

————. *The Hundred Years' War.* San Diego, 1994.

Madison, Lucy F. *Joan of Arc.* New York, 1995.

McGraw, Eloise. *The Striped Ships.* (F) New York, 1991.

Nicole, David. *The Hundred Years' War.* Livonia, MI, 1992.

————. *The Crusades.* Livonia, MI, 1992.

Pyle, Howard. *Men of Iron.* (F) New York, 1965.

Sancha, Sheila. *Walter Dragun's Town: Crafts and Trade in the Middle Ages.* New York, 1989.

Scott, Walter. *Ivanhoe* (F) New York, 1964.

Shakespeare, William. *Henry IV, Parts 1 and 2.* (F) New York.

Ventura, Leonor. *The Rise of Trade in Medieval Europe.* Danbury, CT, 1995.

Illustration Credits

Index

Text is indicated in roman type; illustrations are indicated in italic type.

Charles IV, by name (in France) Charles The Fair, or (in Navarre) Charles The Bald (1294–1328), king of France and of Navarre (as Charles I) 1321, *1362*, 1391, *1391*, *1393*

Charles V, byname Charles the Wise, (1338–1380), king of France *1378–1379*, 1379–1380, 1393, 1411, 1422

Charles VI, byname Charles the Well-beloved, or the Mad, king of France (reigned 1380–1422) 1381, *1381*, 1383, *1383*, *1387*, 1412

Charles VII, byname Charles the Well-served, or the Victorious, king of France (reigned 1422–1461) 1376, 1381, 1383–1386, 1412, *1416*

Charles VIII (1470–1498), king of France 1398

Charles the Bald. *See* Charles IV

Charles of Anjou, brother of the French king Saint Louis IV *1348–1349*, 1349

Charles the Bold, French Charles Le Téméraire (1433–1477), last of the great dukes of Burgundy (1467–1477) 1420, 1422, *1422*

Charles the Simple, king of West Francia 1323

Cherbourg 1386

China 1396

Chingiz (Ghengis) Khan 1404

Chinon 1385

Christ 1340, *1352*, *1365*, 1369, 1374, 1407

Christendom 1312, 1314, 1340, 1354, 1366

Christian
- church 1307
- emperor 1360

Christianity 1323, 1368–1369, 1374, 1392, 1410, 1412

Cistercian order 1307

Cistercians 1307

Citeaux 1307

City charter 1319

City-states 1317

Clarendon Constitution 1326

Clemens V, pope 1407

Clement III, original name Paolo Scolari (?–1191), pope (reigned 1187–1191) 1338

Clement V, original name Bertrand de Got (c.1260–1314), pope (reigned 1305–1314) 1356, 1363, *1363*

Clement VII, original name Giulio de Medici (1478–1534), pope (reigned 1523–1534) 1366

Clergy 1314, 1316, 1323, *1342*, 1353, 1356, 1358, 1365, 1368, 1371, 1381, 1392, 1402

Cologne 1307, 1372, 1391

Colonnas 1394

Colony 1408

Commoners 1325, 1392

Communal government 1312–1313, 1315

Commune 1310, 1313–1314, 1317, 1335

Concordat of Worms 1335. *See also* Worms

Condottieri (mercenaries) 1395–1396.

Confessor 1324, 1328

Coniuratio 1310

Conrad 1333, 1349

Conrad IV, German king from 1237 and king of Sicily from 1251 1349

Constance, heiress of the Norman kingdom of Sicily 1338, *1366*, 1368, 1392

Constantinople 1339, *1339*, 1344–1345, *1350*, 1387

Consuls 1313, 1316

Copenhagen 1402

Coronation 1343, 1348, *1379*, 1392, 1418, 1421

Corsica 1312

Council of
- Basel, held in 1431; Pope Martin tried to sabotage it in vain 1368
- Ferrara, ecumenical council of the Roman Catholic church (1438–1445) in which the Latin and Greek churches tried to reach agreement on their doctrinal differences and end the schism between them 1368
- Pavia, called by Pope Martin in 1423, asserting papal supremacy in all matters ecclesiastical 1368

Courtrai 1317

Cracow 1402, 1410

Credit industry 1307

Crusades 1369

Crusaders 1308, 1338–1339, *1339*, 1344, 1357

Cyprus 1407

Danegeld 1323

Danish 1343, 1400–1401, 1408–1410

Danzig 1408

Denmark 1323, 1343, 1399, *1399–1400*, 1401–1402, 1408–1409

Diet 1335, 1337

Dijon 1412, *1412*, 1416, 1418, 1420

Dominicans 1314

Dominium mundi 1340, 1344–1345, 1352, 1356, 1368

Duke William 1324, 1328

Duomo (Cathedral of Milan) 1397

Easter 1350

Edward III, byname Edward of Windsor, king of England (reigned 1327–1377) 1308, *1376*, 1376–1377, 1379, *1380*, 1381

Egypt 1348, 1354, *1369–1370*

Eidgenossenschaft 1390

England 1321, *1321–1322*, 1323–1329, *1324–1325*, *1330*, 1332, *1337*, 1344, 1352–1354, 1356, 1358–1359, *1364*, 1366, 1369, 1375, *1375–1377*, 1377, 1379, *1380*, 1381, 1383, *1385*, 1386–1387, 1400, 1412, 1418

Eric II, king of Norway 1401

Eric of Pomerania, king of Sweden (1412–1434) 1401, 1408–1409

Ethelred the Unready, king of the English 978–1013; 1014–1016; an ineffectual ruler who failed to prevent the Danes from overrunning England *1322*, 1323–1324

Eugenius III, original name Bernard of Pisa, pope reigned *See page 14*

Eugenius IV, original name Gabriele Condulmer (c.1383–1447), pope (reigned 1431–1447) 1368

Eunuchs 1346

Europe 1303–1304, 1306–1310, 1317–1318, 1320, 1324, 1326–1328, *1336*, 1338, 1345, 1352, 1357–1359, *1358*, 1369–1370, *1371*, 1387–1388, *1388*, 1392, 1399, 1401, 1407–1408, *1409*, 1411, 1414–1416, *1414*

Everlasting Union 1390

Excommunication 1317, 1347–1348, 1366, 1368

Fairs 1304–1307, 1357

Far East 1414

Farming 1303, 1359, 1400

Feudal system 1308, 1316, 1332, 1335, 1338, 1358, 1361, 1418

Feudalism 1319, 1335

Fiefdom 1337, 1384, 1418

Filippo Maria *1397–1398*, 1398

First Crusade *1333*, 1406

Flanders 1304–1305, 1317, 1339, 1354, 1375, 1377–1378, 1412, 1420

Flemish *1319*, 1330, *1358*, 1362, 1377, *1404*

Florence 1312, 1364, *1368*, 1395–1396, 1414, 1422

Foljungar dynasty 1402

Fourth Crusade 1339, 1344

Fourth Lateran Council, held in 1215; an elaborate Crusade plan repeating earlier prohibitions on the transport of military supplies to Muslims 1369

France 1305, 1307, *1311*, 1316–1317, 1321, 1323, 1326–1327, *1328*, 1329–1330, 1332, 1337, *1342*, 1343, *1347*, 1348, 1350, 1352–1354, 1356, *1356–1357*, 1358–1359, 1363–1364, *1364*, 1366, 1369–1372, 1374–1375, *1375–1376*, 1377–1381, *1378–1381*, 1383–1384, *1383*, 1386–1387, *1386–1387*, 1392, 1398, 1406–1407, 1411–1412, *1416*, 1418, 1420

Francesco Sforza, condottiere who played a crucial role in fifteenth–century Italian politics and duke of Milan *1397*, 1398

Francis of Assisi, original name Francesco di Pietro di Bernardone (1181/82–1226); canonized July 15, 1228; founder of the Franciscan orders 1314, *1315*

Franconia 1321

Frankfurt 1318

Frederick I, byname Frederick Barbarossa (Italian: Redbeard), Frederick of Hohenstaufen (c.1123–1190), duke of Swabia (as Frederick III, 1147–1190) and German king and Holy Roman emperor (1152–1190) 1317, *1333*, *1334*, *1335–1338*, *1340*, 1388

Frederick II (1194–1250), king of Sicily (1197–1250), duke of Swabia (as Frederick VI, 1228–1235), German king (1212–1250), and Holy Roman emperor (1220–1250) 1340, *1346*, *1348*, 1354, 1388, 1394, 1404, 1420

Frederick III (1415–1493), Holy Roman emperor from 1452 and German king

Poland (1384–1399) 1410

Jagiello, Vladislav, grand duke of Lithuania (as Jogaila, 1377–1401) and king of Poland (1386–1434), who joined two states that became the leading power of eastern Europe 1410

Jerusalem *1338*, 1339, 1344, *1346*, 1348, 1370, *1387*, 1406

Jesus Christ *1365*, 1369

Jews 1307, 1355–1356, 1369–1372, *1369*, *1371*, *1373–1374*, 1374, 1402, 1415

Joan of Arc (French Jeanne d'Arc) peasant girl who, believing that she was acting under divine guidance, led the French army in a momentous victory at Orléans that repulsed an English attempt to conquer France during the Hundred Years' War 1383–1386, *1383*, *1385*

Joanna, wife of Philip the Fair 1422

John, byname Lackland (French Jean Sans Terre), (1167–1216), king of England (1199–1216); in a war with the French king Philip II, he lost Normandy and almost all his other possessions in France *1328*, 1330, 1332, *1342*, 1344, *1348*, 1352, *1360*, 1367–1368, *1377*, 1378–1379, 1381, *1383*, 1386, 1383, 1403, 1406–1407, *1407*, 1412, *1413*

John the Good (reigned 1350–1364) *1377*, 1379, *1407*

Journeyman 1320

Judaism 1369–1370, 1372

Jura 1421

Kabbalism 1373

Kalmar 1401, 1408–1409

Kalonymus 1372–1373

Khan, Genghis. *See* Chingiz Khan

King
- Haakon IV, byname Haakon the Old, king of Norway (1217–1263) who consolidated the power of the monarchy, patronized the arts, and established Norwegian sovereignty over Greenland and Iceland 1400
- Ottokar, king of Bohemia 1392
- Owl, byname of Philip IV 1354, *See* Philip IV.
- Sweyn Forkbeard, briefly king of England (reigned 1013–1014) 1323

Kraków 1402, 1410

Lagny 1305

Landowners 1307, 1310, 1318–1319, 1361, 1379, 1391–1392

Langton, Stephen (d. 1228), English cardinal whose appointment as archbishop of Canterbury precipitated King John's quarrel with Pope Innocent III and played an important part in the Magna Carta crisis 1344

Languedoc 1378

League of General Welfare 1420

Leaning Tower 1310

Legal system 1370

Legnano. *See* Battle of Legnano

Lent 1305

Liegnitz. *See* Battle of Liegnitz

Limburg 1413

Lithuania 1391, 1410

Loire 1383

Lombard League 1338

Lombards 1308, 1369

Lombardy 1305, 1307, 1317, 1337, 1340, 1349, 1392, 1397–1398

London 1318, 1323–1324, *1377*, 1378, 1381, 1391, 1406, 1416

Lorraine 1384–1385, 1422

Lothar III (1075–1137), German king (1125–1137) and Holy Roman emperor (1133–1137) 1333

Louis IV, byname Louis d'outremer (Louis from Overseas) (921–954), king of France (reigned 936–954) 1349, 1391

Louis VI, byname Louis the Fat, (1081–1137), king of France (reigned 1108–1137) 1328

Louis VII, byname Louis the Younger (c.120–1180), Capetian king of France who pursued a long rivalry, marked by recurrent warfare and continuous intrigue, with Henry II of England 1328

Louis IX, also called Saint Louis (1214–1270), king of France (reigned 1226–1270), most popular of the Capetian monarchs; he led the Seventh Crusade to the Holy Land 1248–1250 and died on another crusade to Tunisia *1350*, *1352–1354*, 1354

Louis XI, king of France (reigned 1461–1483) 1420, 1422

Lowlands 1418

Lubeck 1402

Lucerne 1390

Lugdunensis 1412

Luxembourg *1390*, 1391, 1413

Lyons 1347

Magna Carta 1330, *1342*, 1344, 1353

Magnus the Lawmender, Haakon's son and successor, Magnus VI (reigned 1263–1280) 1400

Mainz 1371–1372, 1391

Manfred, half-brother of Conrad IV 1349–1350

Mantua 1395

Marcel, Etienne 1379

Margaret (of Denmark) (1353–1412), regent of Denmark (from 1375), of Norway (from 1380), and of Sweden (from 1389), who, by diplomacy and war, pursued dynastic policies that led to the Kalmar Union (1397) 1401

Marienburg 1407

Market economy 1304

Marketplaces 1313

Marseilles 1366

Martin V, original name Oddo, or Oddone, Colonna (1368–1431), pope (reigned 1417–1431) *1366*, 1368, *1368*

Martyrs 1372

Mary, heiress to Burgundy *1322*, 1393, 1421–1422

Masons 1310, 1320

Masterpiece 1320

Maximilian, son of Frederick III 1393, 1421–1422

Mediterranean 1350, 1395

Mendicant 1314

Messiah 1369

Metropolis 1345

Michael Paleologus (1261), king of Nicaea 1339, 1384

Middle Ages 1303, 1306–1308, 1310, *1317*, 1318, 1320–1321, 1326, 1343, 1357–1358, 1369, *1370*, 1387, 1395, 1399, 1414–1415, *1421*

Milan *1334*, 1337, 1395–1398, *1397–1398*

Militia 1325, 1407

Monasteries 1307, 1314, 1407

Money changers 1305–1307, *1371*

Moneylending 1307–1308

Mongols 1387, 1403–1404

Monks 1307, 1314, 1406

Monotheism 1369

Mortarers 1320

Moses (fl. c. fourteenth century BC), brother of Aaron, who led the Israelites out of Egypt 1345, 1374

Muslim 1308, *1311*, *1338*, 1346, 1357

Namur 1413

Naples 1350, 1366, 1394, 1398

Narbonne 1372

Navarre *1356*, 1379

Netherlands 1393, 1402, 1412, 1418, 1420, 1422

Neva 1403

Nevsky; Alexander. *See* Alexander Nevsky

New Monastic Orders 1306, 1314, 1406

Nicaea 1339

Nobility 1308, 1322, 1327, 1335, *1342*, 1353, 1358, 1361–1362, 1377, 1379, *1385*, 1387–1388, 1390–1392, 1402, 1418

Noblemen 1327, 1363, 1402, 1407, 1409

Norman *1323–1324*, 1324–1325, 1327, 1338, 1340, 1342, 1345, 1347, 1349–1350

- Empire 1349–1350

Normandy 1323–1325, 1327, 1329, *1348*, 1378, 1381, 1386

Normans 1323–1325, *1323*, 1327, 1340

Norsemen 1323, 1325

North America 1401

Nortmann 1323

Norway 1323–1324, 1399–1401, *1399*, 1408–1409

Novgorod 1391, 1403–1404, 1406

Odo Colonna. *See* Martin V

Olaf IV (c.1099–1115), king of Norway (1103–1115), illegitimate son of King Magnus III the Barefoot 1409

Olaf the Holy; also known as Olaf of Norway; the first Christian king (reigned 1015–1030) 1399

Old Testament 1370, 1374, *1374*

Oligarchy 1313

Orkneys 1400

Orsinis 1394

Osimo 1396

Otto I, byname Otto the Great, German king (from 936), and Holy Roman emperor (962–973) 1303, 1321

Otto III (980–1002), German king and Holy Roman emperor 1331

Otto IV, also called Otto of Brunswick (c.1175/1182–1218), German king and Holy Roman emperor 1340, 1342

Otto the Great. *See* Otto I

Ottokar *1388*, 1392

Ottoman Empire 1364

Padua 1395

Paleologus. *See* Michael Paleologus

Palermo 1345, 1349–1350

Palestine *1333*, 1348, 1374, 1403

Papacy 1337, 1340, 1345, 1348, 1352, 1356, 1363–1364, 1368, 1418, 1422

Papal
- city 1314, 1396
- States 1340, 1342

Paris 1318, 1320–1321, 1328, 1332, 1366, 1372, 1375, 1378–1381, 1383, 1385–1386, 1412, 1416

Patay 1385

Patriarchs 1398

Pavia, *See* Council of Pavia

Peace of Basel, declared on Sept. 22, 1499, with Maximilian unofficially recognizing Swiss independence 1390

Peasants 1307–1308, 1310, 1379, 1381, 1402, 1418, 1421

Pedro de Luna. *See* Benedict XIII

Pentateuch 1370, *1372*

Persians 1339

Peter of Aragon 1350, 1354

Philip II, byname Philip Augustus, (1165–1223), first of the great Capetian kings of medieval France (reigned 1179–1223) 1322, *1328–1329*, 1383

Philip III, byname Philip the Bold, king of France (1270–1285) 1354, *1356*, 1381; 1412; 1416

Philip IV (1268–1314), king of France (1285–1314) and of Navarre, as Philip I (from 1284–1305) ruling jointly with his wife, Joan I of Navarre 1354, *1356*; 1363; 1407; 1418

Philip V, byname Philip the Tall, (c.1293–1322), king of France (from 1316) and king of Navarre (as Philip II, from 1314) 1378

Philip VI, byname Philip of Valois, (1293–1350), first French king of the Valois dynasty 1376–1377, *1376*, *1412*, *1419*

Philip the Bold, *See* Philip III

Philip the Fair, grandson of Louis IX, Philip IV (reigned 1285–1314). *See* Philip IV

Pilgrimages 1415

Pilgrims 1314–1315, 1326–1327, *1327*, 1364, 1406

Pisa 1310, 1312–1313, *1314*, 1315, *1364*, 1367, 1395

Pisans 1312–1313

Plague 1358, *1358*, 1387, 1414–1415, *1414–1415*

Plasterers 1320

Pneumonic plague 1414

Po Valley 1395, 1398

Podestas 1337

Poetry 1372

Poitiers *1377*, 1378, 1381, 1385–1386

Poland *1364*, 1391, 1399, 1402–1404, *1404*, 1408, *1409–1410*, 1410

Pomerania 1390, 1401–1402, 1408–1409

Pope
- Alexander III, *See* Alexander III
- Clement III, *See* Clement III
- Eugenius III, *See* Eugenius III
- Gregory. *See* Gregory VII
- Honorius III, *See* Honorius III
- Innocent III, *See* Innocent III
- Innocent IV, *See* Innocent IV
- Martin V, *See* Martin V
- in Rome 1335, *1364*, 1416

Porto Pisano 1310

Portugal 1366, *1381*

Portuguese 1358

Prelates 1337, 1344, 1354, 1356, 1367–1368, 1402

Provence 1369, 1372–1374

Provins 1305–1306

Prussia 1408, *1409*, 1410

Pyramid 1319

Pyrenees 1380

Queen Isabella. *See* Isabella

Rabbi 1371

Rashi 1371–1372

Rebellion 1329, 1337, 1377, 1379, 1381

Reform movement 1369

Reformation 1391, 1422

Regalia 1380

Reims *1357*, *1383*, 1384–1385

Renaissance 1422

Republic 1315, *1371*

Revolution 1320, 1359

Rhine 1370, 1391

Rhineland 1369, 1372–1373, 1390, 1421

Rhodes 1407

Rhone *1361*, 1363

Richard I, byname Richard the Lion-Heart, or Lion-Hearted, duke of Aquitaine (from 1168) and of Poitiers (from 1172) and king of England, duke of Normandy, and count of Anjou (1189–1199) 1321, 1328, 1331

Richard II, king of England (reigned 1377–1399) *1380*, 1381, *1383*, 1418

Richard the Lion-Hearted. *See* Richard I

Rite of Communion 1369

Robert 1307, 1327

Robertines 1321

Roland. *See* Cardinal Roland

Roman Empire 1303, 1317, 1335, 1343, 1345, 1352, 1363, *1364*, 1370, 1384, 1388, 1391–1393, *1392*

Roman Republic 1315

Rome 1310, 1312, 1314–1317, 1335, 1337, 1342, 1356, 1358, *1360*, *1362*, 1363–1368, *1364*, 1394, *1414*, 1416

Roncaglia 1337

Rouen 1381, 1386, *1386*

Rudolf I (1218-1291), first German king of the Habsburg dynasty *1388*, 1391–1392

Russia 1387, *1399*, 1410

Saint
- Benedict, *See* Benedict XIII
- Catharine, *See* Catherine of Siena
- Louis IV, *See* Louis IV
- Margaret (1556–1586), one of the forty British martyrs who were executed for harbouring priests during the reign of Queen Elizabeth I of England 1384

Saladin, Arabic: Salah Ad-Din Yusuf Ibn Ayyub (Righteousness of the Faith, Joseph, Son of Job): (1137/38–1193), Muslim sultan of Egypt, Syria, Yemen, and Palestine, founder of the Ayyubid dynasty, and the most famous of Muslim heroes *1333*, *1338*, 1339

Sarai 1404

Sardinia 1312

Saxon 1338

Saxony 1334, 1390–1391

Scandinavia 1391, 1399, 1408, 1410

Schaffhausen 1390

Schism 1358, 1366, 1368, 1422

Scotland 1353, *1364*, 1366, 1400

Second Lateran Council, where Pope Eugenius III (1145–1153) declared Arnold of Brescia a heretic, thus making him an outlaw 1316

Semites 1371

Senate 1313, 1315–1317

Serfs 1308, 1318–1319, 1335, *1410*

Sforza; Francesco, *See* Francesco Sforza

Shetland Islands 1400

Shlomo Yitzaki (1040–1105), renowned medieval French commentator on the Bible and Talmud (the authoritative Jewish compendium of law, lore, and commentary) 1371

Sicilian
- Empire 1347, 1350
- Vespers 1350

Sicily 1338, 1340, 1343, 1345, *1346*, 1348–1350, 1392, 1394

Silesia 1402, 1404

Simony 1363–1364

Slavs 1402

Soil exhaustion 1304

Solothurn 1390

Somme 1386

Spain 1357, *1364*, *1367*, 1369, 1387, 1392–1393, 1398, *1406*, 1422

Spider, nickname for the inscrutable King Louis XI 1420

Stamford Bridge 1325

States-General 1379, 1418, *1419*, 1420, 1422

Stockholm 1402, *1404*

Stonecutters 1320

Sultan of Egypt 1348

Swabia 1340, 1342, 1390

Swabian League 1390

Sweden 1399, 1401–1402, *1404*, 1408–1409, *1408*

Swedish 1402, *1402*, 1409

Swiss 1368, 1390, 1421–1422
- Confederation 1390
- League 1390
Switzerland 1390, 1412
Synod 1356

Talmud 1370–1373
Tapestry 1323–1324, 1404
Taxes 1308, *1325*, 1327, 1337, 1344,
 1347, 1354, 1356, 1363, 1397, 1420
Technology 1304
Templars *1344*, 1355–1356, 1407
Teutonic 1399, 1403–1404, 1408,
 1410
Textile production 1304
Third Crusade *1330*, *1333*, 1338–1339
Three-field system 1304
Tiber 1315, 1317
Torah *1370*, 1374
Tours 1306, 1386
Traders 1305, *1388*
Treaty of
- Arras (1435) 1386, 1412
- Hagnenau (1330) 1391
- Stralsund (1370) 1408
Trier 1391, 1421
Troyes 1305–1307, 1371, 1383
Tunis *1353*, 1354
Turkey 1338
Turks 1368, 1387, 1396, 1407
Tuscany 1395, 1398
Tyler; Walter. *See* Wat Tyler

Unterwalden 1390
Upper Germany 1412
Uri 1390
Utrecht 1413

Valdemar (d. 1275), Swedish king of
 the Foljungar dynasty 1402
Valois 1376, 1398, 1412, *1419*
Van Artevelde; Jacob
Vassals 1319, 1321, 1323, 1326–1327,
 1329, 1332–1333, 1335, 1339, 1344,
 1353, 1387–1388, 1391, 1418
Vatican 1314, 1364
Venetian 1306, 1339, *1418*
Venice 1312, 1339, *1373*, 1395–1396,
 1396, 1398, 1414
Verona 1395
Vienna 1409
Viking 1303, 1323, 1325
Viscontis 1396–1398
Vistula River 1409
Vita apostolica 1314
Volga 1404

Waiblingen 1333
Waldemar IV (Atterdag), king of
 Denmark (elected 1340) 1408
Wales 1353
Wat Tyler, byname of Walter Tyler
 (d.1381), leader of the Peasants
 Revolt of 1381, the first great popular
 rebellion in English history 1381
Weavers 1304
Welf 1333–1334
Western Europe 1338
Westminster Abbey 1327

William the Conqueror, byname
 William the Bastard, duke of
 Normandy (as William II) from 1035
 and king of England from 1066
 1324, 1327
Wladislaw IV, Polish king (reigned
 1306–1333) 1402
Worms 1335, 1338, 1371–1372

Yeshiva 1371–1372
York 1325–1326

Zeeland 1413
Zug 1390
Zurich 1390

Text is indicated in roman type; illustrations are indicated in italic type.